HAPPY BIRTH DAY.

$4.50

DEAR CAROL,

may god BLESS you and
keep you ~ may his FACE
SHINE UPON you and GIVE you PEACE.

101 VEGETARIAN DELIGHTS

love,
Kathy.
1997.

BY LILY CHUANG
and CATHY MCNEASE

ILLUSTRATED BY SHELL HODGIN

The Shrine of the Eternal Breath of Tao
College of Tao and Traditional Chinese Healing
Santa Monica, California

DISCLAIMER

This cookbook is intended to provide healthy and healing recipes, to the best of the authors' knowledge and experiences. If you use the recipes outlined to treat serious health conditions, we suggest that you seek the guidance of an experienced Oriental medical doctor to properly diagnose your problem and supervise your diet. Whenever experimenting with a "new" food, always use in a small quantity in the event of an allergic reaction.

Library of Congress Cataloging-in-Publication Data

Chuang, Lily.
　　101 vegetarian delights / by Lily Chuang and Cathy McNease : illustrated by Shell Hodgin.
　　　p.　cm.
　　Includes index.
　　ISBN 0-937064-52-1 : $12.95
　　1. Vegetarian cookery. 2. Cookery, Chinese. I. McNease, Cathy. II. Title. III. Title: One hundred one vegetarian delights. IV. Title: One hundred and one vegetarian delights.
TX837.C465 1992　　　　　　　　　　　　　　91-41184
641.5'636--dc20　　　　　　　　　　　　　　　　CIP

ACKNOWLEDGEMENT

We wish to thank all of the students who participated in the creation of these recipes in our cooking classes. Thanks to Shell Hodgin for contributing her time and talents to our beautiful illustrations. Thanks to our families and friends for your loving support. And a special thanks to our computer whiz, Charles Blythe, for creating our layout.

Lily Chuang
Cathy McNease

CONTENTS

FORWARD

I am thrilled to have the opportunity to introduce Lily and her marvelous vegetarian delights. You will be amazed at the exotic and delicious feasts she has gathered in 101 VEGETARIAN DELIGHTS.

Lily is a skillful and imaginative cook. In these pages she shares her craft and creativity with us as she chops, blends and prepares fresh foods and spices into gourmet meals.

When Lily shows us how to do it...it's easy and delicious. So when we follow her clear and precise recipes and cooking directions, we too can benefit from the balanced and nutritious meals she helps us create.

My clients who keep to a vegetarian diet are blessed with clear and supple skin; while enjoying good health and vigourous well-being. Men and women come to me to maintain youthful appearances. I am delighted to now have Lily's cookbook to recommend to them for that healthy, vibrant glow from within.

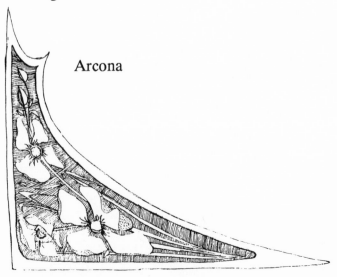

Arcona

PREFACE

Nature is the greatest teacher. Watch the cycle of a tree through a year of seasons. The tree will teach you a lot about appropriateness. In the springtime the tree's energy is moving out into the new buds and leaves. By summer the energy is in the fruits. After the harvest in the fall, the tree sends its energy more inward; by winter, the tree is storing its energy deep in its roots, awaiting the spring thaw. So should our energy follow.

With Nature as their teacher, the ancient wise ones observed foods and how they affected the eater. Through many generations, these observations were systematized and today are a portion of the body of knowledge known as Traditional Chinese Medicine. It comes to us as an example of healthy living and eating that has been tried and tested for thousands of years. (For more detailed information, refer to THE TAO OF NUTRITION by Maoshing Ni and Cathy McNease.)

Balance is the key. Foods are classified as to their overall energies and properties along several continuances: warming/cooling, drying/lubricating, building/detoxifying, etc. Imbalances are treated with the appropriate opposite. For example, summer heat problems are benefitted by cooling foods such as watermelon, cabbage or mung beans. Chills and cold conditions need warming foods, like ginger, pepper or scallions.

Seasonal eating is of utmost importance to good health. Our summer diet should include more cooling fruits and vegetables, while winter fare should be more warming and building. Choose local seasonal produce to attune yourself to the environment.

Traditional Chinese nutrition teaches us to use grains and seeds as the heart of our diet throughout the year, and especially throughout seasonal changes. The subtle sweetness of grains is very nourishing to the center of our being. Rice porridge is greatly therapeutic and easy to digest. Herbs and healing foods are often added to the porridge.

A vegetarian diet is a gentle way of life with both physical and spiritual benefits, providing a wonderful sense of calmness. The Oriental tradition provides us with some helpful methods to assure that the diet is well balanced and nourishing, based on grains, beans, mushrooms, seaweeds, and an abundance of fresh vegetables and fruits.

Those adhering to a vegetarian diet as strict Buddhists or those practicing celibacy should omit the garlic, onions and chives from any recipes that include them. These foods are considered to be sexually stimulating and thus inappropriate in some spiritual pursuits. Some Buddhists and Hindu sects would also refrain from eating eggs because they too closely resemble animals.

Appropriate choices move us toward balance, further our development, and bring a sense of well being. Each meal is an opportunity to harmonize with Nature.

Cathy McNease

APPETIZERS AND FINGER FOODS

SIMPLE CHINESE APPETIZER

daikon, large one
1 T. honey or any kind of syrup
1 T. miso
small piece ginger, finely grated
juice of 1 lemon
salt, a pinch
1/4 t. toasted sesame oil

Clean daikon then slice thinly. Put into a big bowl with a pinch of salt and mix well. Set aside for 30 minutes.

Squeeze out the water from the daikon using both hands, getting as much water out as possible. Then put into another bowl and add the rest of the ingredients, mixing well. Set aside for 30 minutes and let the daikon absorb the seasonings well. It is then ready to serve.

CHINESE SEAWEED DUMPLINGS
Serves 6-8

DOUGH:
1 1/2 c. whole wheat pastry flour
1 1/2 c. unbleached white flour
   Or 3 c. unbleached white flour
1 c. plus 1 T. water

FILLING:
small handful hiziki seaweed, soaked and chopped
1 package tofu cake, grated or finely chopped
6 - 10 Chinese mushrooms, soaked, chopped
5 - 6 fresh water chestnuts, finely chopped
2 - 3 carrots, finely grated
2 - 3 leaves cabbage, finely chopped
ginger, finely grated
toasted sesame oil
soy sauce
wheat flour, a little bit (optional if filling is too moist)

Combine the dough ingredients and knead until smooth. Set aside and prepare the filling. Combine the filling ingredients and lightly saute; if it is watery add the flour.

Roll the dough into a long, thin roll (about 1 inch diameter). Cut into 1/2 inch rounds; flatten with a rolling pin trying the make the edges thinner than the middle. Put a spoonful of the filling in the middle, fold in half and pinch the edges together. Try not to get any filling along the edges or it will not stick. Place the finished dumplings on a floured plate.

When you have made about a dozen dumplings, cook them in one of the following ways:
1. Steam on a plate for about 10 minutes.

2. Put into boiling water for a few minutes, until water comes to a boil again.

3. Fry on both sides in a lightly oiled pan for just a few minutes; then add a little water or mushroom soak water, cover and cook for a few minutes.

VEGETABLE MUSHU AND NORI
Serves 6

6 wheat tortillas
plum, prune, or any kind of fruit jam
4 pieces baked tofu, thinly sliced
5 - 6 Chinese mushrooms, soaked and thinly sliced
1 handful of each of the following, cut into strips:
  cabbage, carrots, and jicama
6 sheets toasted nori seaweed
oil and soy sauce, a little bit
cilantro and grated ginger

In a pan add a little bit of oil and cook Chinese mushrooms on a low flame until tender. Turn heat to medium and add tofu cake and carrots; cook for 5 minutes, then add cabbage and jicama and stir fry them for 2 minutes. Turn off flame and add soy sauce, cilantro and ginger.

Lay one sheet of nori on plate, followed by a tortilla with jam spread over it. Then put some tofu, mushrooms, and vegetables in the middle. Roll up the tortilla and nori like a burrito.

KOMBU SEAWEED ROLLS
Serves 6 - 8

6 - 8 Chinese mushrooms, soaked and sliced
1 package baked tofu, finely sliced
1 long strip kombu seaweed, soaked until soft
cabbage leaves steamed whole (optional)

Saute mushrooms and tofu in a little sesame oil, soy sauce and grated ginger.

Spread out kombu on the cutting board. Put about 3 T. of the tofu-mushroom mixture on the kombu, then wrap it like a roll. When the filling is closed inside, cut of kombu and tie with a string. Continue making these rolls until the kombu is all used. Put the rolls in a steamer and steam for 30 minutes over a medium flame.

*After removing the strings the rolls can be rolled in the cabbage leaves.

SIMPLE PICKLE

equal portions of daikon and kolhrabi
cilantro
toasted sesame oil
lemon juice
honey

Cut daikon and kolhrabi into thin matchsticks.

Sprinkle a pinch of salt over the vegetables and let set 15
minutes. Then squeeze out the water and add chopped
cilantro.

Season with a few drops of toasted sesame oil (or any kind
of oil), a little lemon juice and if you like it sweet, a little
honey.

* A delicious salad can be made with this pickle and hair
seaweed or other seaweed.

"PEARL" BALLS
Serves 5

Choose one of the following and soak overnight:
  1. 1/2 c. brown sweet rice or white sweet rice
  2. 1/2 c. millet
  3. 1/2 c. wheat berries

2-3 Chinese mushrooms, soaked and finely chopped
1 small carrot, parsnip or gobo root, finely grated
1/3 c. to 1/2 c. flour
1 t. grated ginger
1 t. white pepper (optional)
1 t. soy sauce and oil
1 square baked tofu or 1/4 block tempeh, finely chopped

After soaking the grain overnight, drain off the water and spread out on a large dish. Mix Chinese mushrooms, vegetables, flour, and seasoning well, then make small balls, using both hands. Roll over the grains until the balls are covered. Place the "pearl" balls on a plate and steam over a medium flame: millet-30 minutes, rice-40 minutes, wheat berries-60 minutes.

While the "pearl" balls steam, you may prepare one of the following garnishes to roll the balls in when done steaming:
  1. cilantro, finely chopped
  2. nori seaweed, torn into small pieces
  3. brown or black sesame meal (made in the blender)

SEAWEED APPETIZERS
Makes 30 pieces

1 bag frozen soybean film
5-10 Chinese mushrooms, soaked and sliced
1 package baked tofu, cut into matchsticks
handful coarsely grated carrots
handful finely chopped cabbage
1/2 handful finely chopped mustard stem pickle, rinsed
handful hiziki, soaked
a little toasted sesame oil
1 T. grated ginger
a litte finely chopped cilantro
5 sheets of nori, each cut into 6 pieces

Saute Chinese mushrooms until they are tender. Then add
carrots and cook for a few minutes, followed by cabbage,
tofu and hiziki for a few minutes. Turn off heat and add
ginger, pickle, sesame oil and cilantro. Mix well then set
aside.

Cut soybean film sheets into thirds. Put two tablespoons
of filling in the middle. Fold over the sides and begin to
roll up from one end. Use egg yolk for glue to seal up the
end. Wrap each appetizer in a small piece of nori, using
egg yolk once again to make it stick shut. Lightly fry on
both sides in a very small amount of oil.

* These appetizers can also be steamed insteaed of frying.
Steam for a few minutes before putting on the nori.

AZUKI BEAN SPREAD

1 c. azuki beans, soaked in 1 c. water
1/2 lb. kaboche squash, cut into large chunks
1 - 2 T. miso
1 T. grated ginger
2 T. oil

Put squash on top of azuki beans and steam until the azuki beans get soft. Mash them and mix with miso, ginger and oil.

This spread can be used on bread, tortillas, pocket breads, etc.

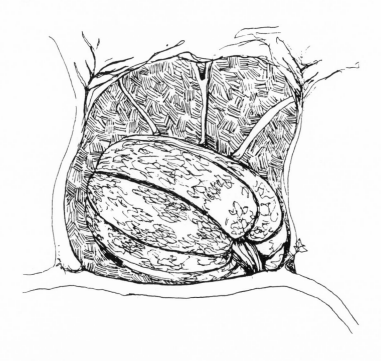

STEAMED CILANTRO PATTY

Serves 5-6

1 c. wheat berries
1/2 c. garbonzo beans or pinto beans
1/2 c. couscous
1/2 c. oat bran
1/2 handful grated gobo root or finely chopped cabbage
1/2 handful grated carrot
1 handful finely chopped cilantro
1 T. oil

Optional:
3 - 4 Chinese mushrooms, soaked and chopped
ginger, grated

Soak wheat berries and beans together in 2 c. of water for a few hours or overnight. Bring to a boil, then simmer until soft on a very low flame. Turn off flame and mix with couscous (while hot). Set aside and let sit for 10 minutes while the couscous absorbs the liquid and gets soft. Then mix with the rest of the ingredients.

Use hands to form into patties or balls. Put them on a plate with space in between them and steam over high flame for 10 minutes. When serving, if the taste is too plain, you may dip them in soy sauce, ketchup or mayonnaise.

* The patty can be fried in a little oil over medium flame on both sides; it takes about 8 - 10 minutes.

** If you don't have time to soak beans and wheat ahead of time use the following method:

Put beans and wheat in boiling water for 1 minute then turn off flame, cover and let set for 1/2 hour. This will do the same thing as the soaking process.

PESTO

2 c. fresh basil, parley and chives; or all basil
sprig fresh rosemary
1/3 c. olive oil
1 T. Bragg's Liquid Aminos
1 clove fresh garlic
1 c. (or as much as will blend) pinenuts

Blend first 5 ingredients. Add pinenuts until blender will
not blend anymore. Serve over noodles or steamed grains,
or as a dip for crackers or celery sticks.

CATHY'S VEGETABLE MUSHU

SAUCE
2 c. mushroom soak water
3 T. dark miso
1/4 - 1/2 c. brown rice syrup
toasted sesame oil
ginger, finely grated
4 - 6 T. arrowroot or kuzu, dissolved in cold water

Blend ingredients. Heat until thickened. It should be a very thick sauce; if not, add more thickener. If arrowroot is used, do not boil.

FILLING:
2 c. Chinese mushrooms, soaked and thinly sliced
1 package baked tofu, sliced small
1/4 cabbage, shredded
small jicama
3 carrots, grated
ginger, finely grated
1 c. lily flowers, soaked and tough stems removed
1/4 c. sauce for seasoning

Cook together in as little water as possible. When done add the 1/4 c. sauce

PANCAKE:
3 eggs
1 c. water
1/4 c. Chinese mushroom powder (optional)
toasted sesame oil and grated giner
unbleached white flour or whole wheat pastry flour

Beat the eggs, add water, oil, ginger and mushroom powder. Then add enough flour to make a thin batter. Pour

thinly into crepe type pan and cook on both sides until done
(a couple of minutes on each side).

To assemble and serve this, put the filling in a line in the
middle of a pancake and fold over the two sides. Sauce can
be spread inside the pancake, spread on top or simply
served to each guest on the side.

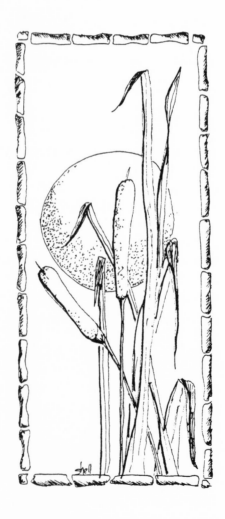

SUCCESSFUL SUSHI

    sheets of toasted nori seaweed
    steamed rice (1/4 c. dry rice per roll)
    carrot sticks, steamed
    cucumber sticks
    pickled ginger slices
    cilantro, chopped
    scallions, chopped
    toasted sesame seed meal (made in blender)
    umeboshi plum paste (optional)

Vegetarian nori rolls are a convenient and delicious treat. A few simple practices make their preparation easy. First, be sure your rice is <u>warm</u> when assembling.

Lay out bamboo sushi mat (or a double thickness of paper towel) and a sheet of toasted nori. Spread a layer of steamed rice over the first 3/4 of nori, totally covering 3/4 of the sheet. Press rice firmly onto nori. In the center of the rice, spread a small amount of umeboshi plum paste, followed by steamed carrot sticks, de-seeded cucumber sticks, pickled ginger, cilantro, scallions, and toasted sesame seed meal.

Roll as tightly as possible. Pack in any rice that falls out of the ends. When cutting, use a wet knife and halve them first, then cut each half into three pieces.

Serve with miso soup.

* Try other filling ingredients like avocado, jicama sticks, steamed celery sticks, fresh basil, etc.

SOUPS, SAUCES & DRINKS

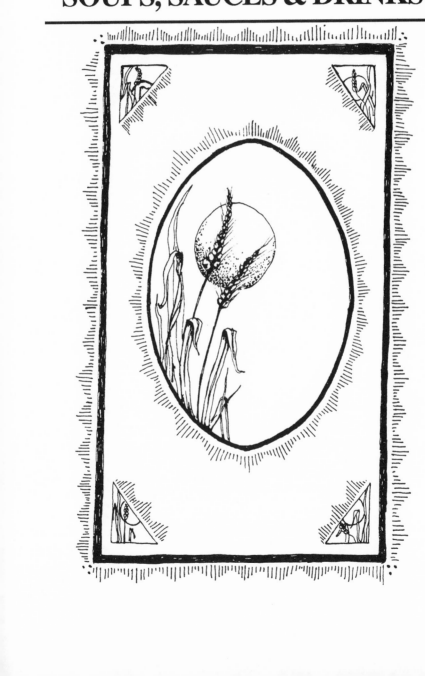

MISO SOUP FOR WINTER

Serves 6 - 8

1 - 2 lb. kaboche squash, cut into bite size cubes
1 - 2 c. skinless peanuts, soaked in 7 - 10 c. water
  overnight or in hot water a few hours
1/8 c. - 1/4 c. miso (any kind), dissolved in a little water
1 - 2 T. ginger, finely grated
cilantro for garnish
1 sheet nori, torn into small pieces
1/2 lb. plain tofu, cut into bite size cubes (optional)

In a soup pot bring peanuts and soaking water to a boil, then turn to low and simmer until tender (about 1 hour). If a pressure cooker is used, it takes only about 30 minutes. Add kaboche squash, turn flame to medium and cook until squash gets tender (about 15 minutes). Add tofu (if used), ginger and miso, and stir for 1 minute. Turn heat off, garnish with pieces of nori and cilantro. Serve hot.

* If you desire a thicker soup, use 7 c. water to soak the peanuts, and perhaps a larger kaboche squash. If soup is too thick, add more water before adding squash.

** Miso is a good seasoning for soup. Always add it in the last minutes of cooking, dissolved in a little water.. There are many kinds of miso, made from soybeans and various different grains. The light colored ones have a lighter flavor; the dark ones are more salty. Use a small amount at first, then add more to taste.

*** Ginger is good to warm up the body, especially in winter. Start with a small amount if you have not used fresh ginger before.

GARBONZO MISO SOUP

Serves 5-6

1 c. dry garbonzo beans soaked overnight in 5-6 c.
  water
2 - 3 T. miso, dissolved in a little water
1 T. grated ginger
cilantro for garnish

Cook the garbonzo beans until soft, about 1 hour (or 1/2
hour in a pressure cooker). When done, mash part of the
beans and add the miso, ginger and cilantro. Serve hot.

TWO MINUTE MISO SOUP

Serves 4-5

4-5 c. soybean milk
1-2 sheets nori, torn into little pieces
1-2 T. miso, dissolved in a little water
1 T. grated ginger
cilantro or chopped celery for garnish
1 small tomato, cut into chunks
1/2 lb. tofu

Bring soy milk to a boil. Then add tomato, tofu, ginger and cook for 2 minutes. Turn off heat and mix in miso. Add nori and garnish with cilantro or celery.

*Variation: Instead of using tomato, substitute 1/4 c. green peas.

CHESTNUT MISO SOUP

Serves 6 - 8

8 oz. dry chestnuts, soaked in 7 c. water
10 inch piece kombu, cut into 1 inch slices and tied into
   knots
5 - 8 Chinese mushrooms, soaked and quartered
2 - 3 T. miso, dissolved in a little water
1 T. grated ginger
cilantro for garnish

Bring chestnuts to a boil with their soak water; add Chinese mushrooms and kombu. Turn to low, simmer until chestnuts are soft. Turn off heat; add miso and ginger and garnish with cilantro.

* To save time this soup can be prepared in a pressure cooker.

MUNG BEAN SOUP

Serves 5 - 6

1/2 c. millet
1 c. mung beans
1 small yam (cleaned or peeled), cut into bite size cubes
1/4 c. brown rice syrup (optional)

Combine millet, mung beans and 7 c. water in a deep pan. Bring to a boil, then turn to low flame and cook until almost tender (about 40 minutes). Now add the yam and continue cooking until all is tender.

Add brown rice syrup if you desire it sweeter.

*Mung beans clear out excess heat, and thus are good to eat during the summer months.

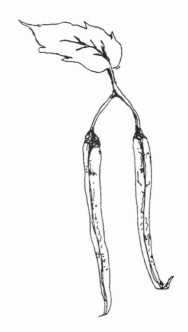

ELEGANT SOUP

Serves 6

4 oz. dried soy bean sticks, soaked until soft and cut into 2
   inch pieces
1/4 lb. tofu, cut into bite size cubes
5-10 Chinese mushrooms, soaked and sliced
5-10 white mushrooms, sliced
1/2 can straw mushrooms
1 small cucumber, peeled, deseeded and cut into chunks
1/2 can baby corn, cut into halves
1 stalk celery, chopped
1/2 handful carrots, thin sliced
pinch of salt
pinch of white pepper

Bring 7 c. of water to a boil. Add soy bean sticks and
Chinese mushrooms and cook for 20 minutes over low
flame. Then add tofu, cucumber and carrots and cook for
5 minutes. Add the remaining ingredients and cook for 1
minute. Turn heat off and add salt and pepper.

* When soaking the dried soy bean sticks, put a plate on
top to hold them under the water, otherwise they will float
to above the water.

TEMPEH NOODLE SOUP

Serves 4 - 6

1 package tempeh, cut into bite-size cubes
5-10 Chinese mushrooms (soaked and quartered) or white
    mushrooms (sliced or quartered)
1/4 lb. noodles, any kind
1 bunch watercress, cleaned and cut in large pieces
handful bean sprouts
a few thin slices of carrot
a few thin slices of ginger
sesame oil, a few drops
soy sauce, a few drops
pinch of salt

In a sauce pan add 8 c. water; bring to a boil. Add tempeh
and Chinese mushrooms and cook for 20 minutes. Then
add noodles and stir well. When noodles are almost done,
turn heat to high and add carrots, bean sprouts, water cress,
ginger, and white mushrooms (if used). Stir well. After a
few minutes, turn off heat, add salt and garnish with soy
sauce and oil.

CREAMY "SILVER EARS" SOUP

Serves 6

1 handful dry white fungus, also known as "silver ears
    mushroom", (Bai Mu Er, 白木耳), soaked and cleaned
1 c. skinless peanuts
8 oz. dry chestnuts
1/2 c. sweet rice
1/2 c. raisins or 10 pitted dates or 15 Chinese jujube dates
    (Da Zao, 大 棗)

After soaking briefly in warm water, clean the white fungus
and cut away the tough stem. Soak the cleaned white
fungus with peanuts, chestnuts and rice and 7-8 c. water
overnight.

Bring water to boil, then add dates or raisins. Boil again
then turn heat to low and simmer until creamy (about 2
hours).

*The quick way is to use a pressure cooker for 1 - 1 1/2
hours.

** To prepare in a slow cooker, bring to a boil then turn to
low and cook overnight.

WHITE MUSHROOM BALL SOUP

Serves 4

MUSHROOM BALLS:
8 oz. white mushrooms, finely chopped
1/2 - 1 t. white pepper
1 T. soy sauce
1 T. toasted sesame oil
1/2 - 3/4 c. white flour
1/2 egg or 1 T. water
little bit of cilantro, finely chopped

1/4 lb. tofu, cut into bite-size cubes
2 T. miso
1 stalk celery, finely chopped
few drops toasted sesame oil

Bring 3 c. water to a boil. Mix together well the mushroom ball ingredients, then form small balls.

One by one drop into the boiling water. When all the balls have been put in, add tofu and miso. When it comes to a boil, turn off heat and garnish with toasted sesame oil and celery.

HAIR SEAWEED SOUP

1/4 oz. hair seaweed, soaked and chopped
1/2 handful dried lily flowers, soaked and stems removed
1 square baked tofu, cut into matchsticks
3-5 Chinese mushrooms, soaked and thinly sliced
1-2 ears black fungus, soaked and sliced
3-4 leaves Napa cabbage, thinly sliced
1/2 handful grated carrot and jicama
2 T. cornstarch or other thickener, mixed with a little
  cold water
pinch of salt
1 t. white pepper (optional)
little bit of cilantro and sesame oil for garnish

Bring 6-8 c. water to a boil and add seaweed, lily flowers, mushrooms, and black fungus. Turn heat to low and simmer until tender. Then add tofu and vegetables, turn heat to high and cook a few minutes. Next, pour in thickener, stir well and add the rest of the ingredients. Garnish with sesame oil and cilantro.

WINTER MELON S

32

Serves 6

1 - 2 lb. winter melon
5 - 10 Chinese mushrooms, soaked and quartered
5 medium size white mushrooms, quartered then mixed
    with 1 T. cornstarch or arrowroot
1/2 lb. tempeh or 1/4 lb. tofu, cut into bite-size cubes
few thin slices ginger
pinch of salt
few drops of toasted sesame oil
cilantro for garnish

Bring 6 - 8 c. water (or Chinese mushroom soak water) to a boil. Add winter melon, ginger, Chinese mushrooms and tempeh (if used). Cook until the melon gets soft (when a fork easily goes through it), about 15 minutes over medium flame. Then add tofu (if used) and white mushrooms (one by one) and stir slowly. When the water comes to a boil again, turn heat off, add pinch of salt, sesame oil and cilantro for garnish.

DAIKON SOUP WITH VEGETARIAN "MEAT BALLS"

VEGETARIAN MEAT BALLS

Dough:
1 c. gluten flour
1 egg
1 T. sesame oil
1 T. soy sauce
1/2 t. white pepper (optional)
2 T. Chinese mushroom powder (optional)

Filling:
2 - 5 Chinese mushrooms, soaked and chopped finely
1 small "ear" black fungus, soaked and chopped finely
soy sauce
sesame oil
ginger, finely grated

Mix together the dough ingredients (if too dry add a little water) and knead well. Form small balls. Combine the filling ingredients. Put filling in the middle of each ball and close. Arrange on plate for steaming, leaving a space between the balls to allow room for them to expand. Steam for one hour over medium flame.

While these are steaming, prepare the soup.

DAIKON SOUP

1 medium daikon, cut into big chunks
5 white mushrooms, sliced
6" piece of kombu seaweed, cut lengthwise into 1/2"wide
    strips and tied into many knots

4 - 5 water chestnuts, cut into bite size pieces
4 - 5 Chinese mushrooms, cut in large pieces
a few bite size cubes of plain tofu
pinch of salt
few drops sesame oil
cilantro for garnish
miso to taste (optional)

Combine daikon, seaweed, Chinese mushrooms, and water chestnuts with 6 - 8 c. boiling water. Turn flame to low and cook until soft (about 1/2 hour). Add white mushrooms and tofu, turn flame to high for 1 minute. Turn off heat. Add a few drops of sesame oil, pinch of salt and garnish with cilantro. Soup can be seasoned with miso if desired.

Add the steamed vegetarian meat balls to the soup.

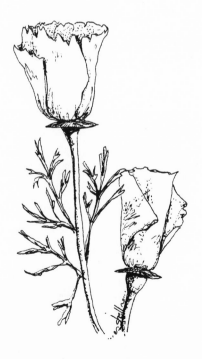

TOFU VEGETABLE STEW

1 8 oz. package dried bean curd sticks
10 Chinese mushrooms, soaked and sliced
1 "ear" black fungus, soaked and sliced
1 8 inch piece kombu, soaked and sliced
2 large carrots, cut into large pieces
1 small daikon, cut into large pieces
1 leek, cut into large pieces
1/4 c. fermented bean curd or miso
1/2 t. toasted sesame oil
1 handful lily bulbs (Bai He, 百 合), soaked (optional)
fresh parsley, cilantro or basil (optional)

Soak tofu skins over night with a plate on top to hold them under the water.

Then, cook them until soft (about 30 minutes) with the soak water and the mushrooms, black fungus, kombu slices, lily flowers, lily bulbs, and fermented bean curd.

When almost done add carrots, daikon and leeks and cook until soft. Turn off fire and add the sesame oil and finely chopped parsley, cilantro or basil.

*This soup can also be seasoned with Chinese 5-spice.

BROTHS:

DETOXIFYING B

Simmer together for 30 minutes:
3 carrot tops and roots
1 beet top and root
1 6" piece of seaweed (any kind)
handful of dandelion greens
6 Chinese mushrooms
4 c. water

Add watercress and simmer 5 more minutes.

HARDY VEGETARIAN BROTH

Simmer together 30 minutes:
10 Chinese mushrooms
1 10" piece kombu or wakame seaweed
1 slice wax gourd peel
4 c. water

PROTEIN BROTH

Simmer together for 30 minutes:
1 handful soy bean sprouts
1 10" piece kombu

ZPACHO

Finely chop the following:
  1 cucumber, de-seeded
  5 - 10 roma (Italian) tomatoes
  1 bell pepper
  1 piece sweet red onion
  2 celery stalks
  fresh parsley, basil, chives, oregano, and cilantro
1 large can of tomato juice
2 T. Bragg's Liquid Aminos
1 T. tamari
1 t. olive oil
1/2 t. toasted sesame oil
pinch garlic powder
pinch herb salt
1/4 t. coriander seed powder
1 small can diced chilis

Combine ingredients and serve as a chilled soup.

LILY FLOWER AND SWEET SQUASH SOUP

1 small winter squash (kaboche, buttercup, butternut,
   or acorn), chopped and deseeded (butternut must be
   peeled)
1 8 inch pieces kombu, soaked and sliced
5 Chinese mushrooms, soaked and sliced
1 piece dried wax gourd peel, soaked and sliced
1 handful dried lily flowers, soaked and stems removed
1 small onion, chopped
3 leaves Napa cabbage, chopped
garbonzo (or other variety) miso, to taste
toasted sesame oil
cilantro for garnish

Combine everything but the cabbage, miso and oil with 10
c. water and simmer 30 minutes or until squash is soft. Add
cabbage and simmer 10 more minutes. Turn off flame and
add about 1/4 c. miso dissolved in a little water and the oil.

Garnish with cilantro

BARLEY MUSHROOM STEW

6 Chinese mushrooms, soaked and sliced
1 slice wax gourd peel, rinsed and chopped
1 8" piece wakame seaweed, rinsed and chopped
1 small kaboche squash, cut into small pieces
1 c. raw, skinless peanuts, soaked overnight
1 small onion, chopped
1 carrot, chopped
1/2 c. barley flakes
miso to taste (about 1/4 c.)
cilantro for garnish

Begin simmering the mushrooms, wax gourd peel and wakame in 10 c. water while preparing the vegetables to make a rich broth.

Add the peanuts, kaboche, carrot, onion and barley flakes. Simmer together until peanuts and squash are soft (about 45 minutes-1 hour). When done turn off flame and add the miso (dissolved in a little broth).

Garnish with cilantro.

PEANUT GRAVY

2 c. mushroom soak water
5 - 10 Chinese mushrooms, soaked and sliced
2 T. peanut butter or cooked peanuts
1 t. rice syrup
ginger, finely grated
6 T. kuzu
1/2 t. toasted sesame oil
4 T. Bragg's Liquid Aminos
pinch of Chinese 5 Spice powder
1 T. miso

Cook the mushrooms in a little of the soak water.

Blend the other ingredients and add to the cooking mushrooms. Cook until thickened, stirring constantly.

Serve over noodles, gluten loaf, or steamed grains. Add chopped cilantro and green onions as a garnish when serving.

COCONUT MILK CURRY

2 stalks broccoli
1 yam
6 Chinese mushrooms, soaked
1 6 inch piece kombu, soaked and sliced thinly

Cook vegetables in a little mushroom soak water until soft.

Blend the following for the curry sauce:
   16 oz. coconut milk
   2 T. arrowroot or sweet rice flour
   2 t. curry powder
   1/2 t. coriander powder
   1/4 t. nutmeg or a pinch of mace
   1/2 t. dry onion granules or powder
   1/2 t. soy sauce
   tops of 2 scallions, chopped

Add to cooked vegetables and heat until thickened. Serve over basmati rice and garnish with fresh herbs like cilantro, basil or parsley.

RICE MILK

This is a very nutritious drink for people with weak stomachs, babies or after surgeries.

1 c. rice
6 c. water

Cook for 2-3 hours, then pour off the "milk" at the top and add a pinch of salt.

*Variations:
1. For those with water retention problems, add a small handful of Job's tears (Yi Yi Ren,薏米) at the beginning of cooking.

2. For those with stomach problems, add a handful of cabbage in the last 5 minutes of cooking and turn flame to high. Then strain off the liquid.

3. For those who are weak, add a handful of spinach in the last 5 minutes of cooking and turn the flame to high. Then strain off the liquid.

ALMOND MILK

Soak a handful of raw almonds in 1 1/2 c. water for several hours. Then grind in blender a few minutes with soak water. Strain out the solids.

The remaining almond milk can be sweetened if desired with rice syrup, maple syrup, honey or carob powder.

*This can be blended with fruits such as banana, papaya or mango.

** Almond milk is delicious over cereal or served as a warm drink.

SOYBEAN (OR BLACK BEAN) MILK

Making soybean milk is very simple. Begin by making a small cotton bag for straining the soymilk. Then prepare as follows:

1. Clean 1 c. soybeans and soak in 2 c. water overnight (or soak in the refreigerator for 2 days for a better taste). Soybeans can be soaked in hot water for a few hours; be sure beans are soft enough to blend.

2. Pour 1/2 of soybeans each time into blender (together with soak water) and enough water to fill blender 80% full. Blend for a few minutes.

3. Prepare large pot (large enough to hold 10 c. liquid). Place cloth bag in pot and pour the blended soybeans into the bag, squeezing out the liquid and saving the pulp in a dish (to be blended later with more water).

4. Repeat steps 2 and 3 with the remaining soybeans. A third blending with the pulp (repeating the process) is optional.

5. Bring the soybean liquid to a boil, stirring often. Boil 10 minutes. Turn down the flame when it gets near boiling so that the soybean milk does not boil over.

The soybean milk can be made thick or thin, depending upon the amount of water used. For 1 c. of dry soybeans you will use between 10 c. and 14 c. of water.

*Black beans can be used for making black bean milk using the same process as making soybean milk. Drinking black bean milk often will strengthen the kidneys.

HERB DRINKS TO LOWER BLOOD PRESSURE

15 grams Chrysanthemum flowers (Ju Hua,菊花)
6 grams Licorice root (Gan Cao, 甘草)
10 grams Ophiopogonas (Mai Men Dong, 麥冬)

Combine herbs with 8 c. water. Simmer in a non-metal pan for 1 hour on low flame, then strain tea.

OR:

10 grams Hawthorn Berries (Shan Zha,山楂)
6 grams Licorice (Gan Cao, 甘草)

Combine herbs with 5 c. water. Simmer in a non-metal pan for 1 hour on low flame, then strain tea.

* The herbs can be boiled one more time, reducing the water to 2 c.

DELICIOUS TEA FOR DIGESTION

1 t. each :
  fennel seeds
  anise seeds
  flax seeds
  fenugreek seeds
  licorice root
1/2 t. peppermint leaves

Simmer the seeds and the licorice root in 4 c. water for 10 minutes. Turn off flame and add the mint; cover and steep another 5 minutes. Strain and serve as an after dinner tea.

GRAIN AND NOODLE DISHES

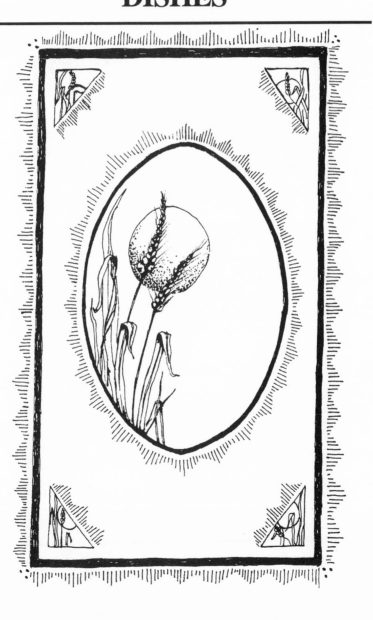

TARO LOAF

Serves 4 - 6

1/2 c. millet
1/2 c. rice
  Soak these in 1 c. water for a few hours

3" piece daikon, bite size cubes
1 medium or 2 small taro roots, bite size cubes
10 Chinese mushrooms, soaked and thin sliced
ginger, grated
1/4 c. oat bran
1/4 c. couscous
oil and soy sauce, to taste

Saute the mushrooms with a little bit of oil; then add the daikon, taro root and a little soy sauce. Mix well and turn heat off. Add 1 c. mushroom soak water then mix with the rest of the ingredients including the grains and their soak water. Set aside for 15 minutes to let the couscous absorb the liquid. Press into a pan or bowl and steam for 1 hour over medium flame.

MUNG BEAN NOODLES WITH TOFU AND SEAWEED

Serves 5 - 10

6 oz. dry mung bean noodles
5 - 8 Chinese mushroom, soaked and sliced
1 handful lily flowers, soaked
1 - 2 "ears" black fungus, soaked
8 - 10 inch piece kombu seaweed, soaked and sliced (or a
    handful hiziki seaweed, cleaned and soaked)
4 squares baked tofu, sliced
1 handful celery slices
2 handfuls cabbage, chopped (red and/or green)
2 handfuls carrot slices
2 handfuls mung bean sprouts
cilantro for garnish
toasted sesame oil
cold pressed oil
soy sauce
grated ginger
curry powder, a little bit (optional)

Soak mung bean noodles in cold or hot water until soft (10
- 20 minutes), then strain. While the mung bean noodles
are soaking, slice the Chinese mushrooms, kombu, and
black fungus.

In a pan add 3 c. water (depending on how soft you like
your noodles), a little sesame oil, cold pressed oil, soy
sauce, ginger and curry powder. Bring to a boil then add
noodles; turn heat to low, stir well, cover and simmer until
noodles get soft and absorb all the seasoning. When noodles are cooked set aside (or put in a big bowl).

In another pan add some water, mushrooms, black fungus, lily flowers and kombu; simmer until everything is tender, then add the sliced tofu and stir well. Add the rest of the ingredients except the cilantro. If pan is not large enough to add the vegetables, they can be cooked separately then mixed with the mushroom mixture. Add oil and soy sauce to taste.

When serving, put the vegetable mixture on the plate, then noodles on top

Garnish with cilantro.

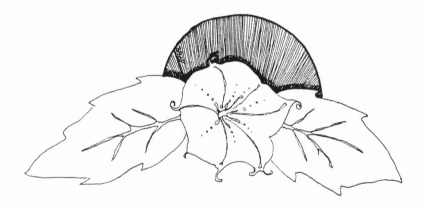

BLACK EYED PEA SAUCE OVER MACARONI

Serves 5-6

1 c. black eyed peas, soaked in 6 c. water
1/2 lb. macaroni
1/2 small kohlrabi or jicama, cut into small cubes
1 small parsnip, cut into small cubes
1 small carrot or 1 c. kaboche squash, cubed
1/2 basket cherry tomatoes or 1 large tomato, cut into
   chunks
1 small potato, cubed
1 stalk celery, finely chopped
5 - 10 white mushrooms, sliced
miso
cilantro

Simmer peas for 1/2 hour on low flame. Then add kohlrabi and potato and cook 10 minutes. Then add parsnips and carrots, turn heat to high and cook until soft. Add tomatoes, celery, white mushrooms and miso, cook for 2 minutes, then turn off flame.

When the pea sauce is almost done, cook the macaroni. Pour off the water and serve the macaroni with the pea sauce poured on top. Garnish with cilantro.

MILLET - TOFU SALAD

Serves 4 - 6

1 c. millet , soaked in 1 c. water
1 small potato, peeled and cut into bite-size cubes
1 lb. tofu, cut into bite-size cubes
mayonnaise, to taste
1 handful each of the following grated vegetables:
  kohlrabi
  carrot
  daikon
  cucumber
cilantro, finely chopped
sesame oil
1 T. grated ginger

In a large bowl combine grated kohlrabi, carrot, daikon, and cucumber. Add a pinch of salt and mix well, then set aside. The salt water will draw out the water.

Steam millet and potato separately until they get tender, or put potato cubes on top of millet and steam together. Cook tofu cubes in boiling water for a few minutes, then strain off the excess water. Mix together well the millet, potato, tofu, cilantro and mayonnaise. Put in the center of a large serving dish.

Squeeze out the water from the grated vegetables, then mix with sesame oil and ginger. Spread this around the millet tofu salad in the center.

AMARANTH AND GRAIN DISH

Serves 4-5

1 c. brown or sweet rice
1/2 c. millet
1/2 c. amaranth
1 t. grated ginger
1 T. miso, dissolved in a little water
1 T. oil or a few drops of toasted sesame oil
a little finely chopped cilantro for garnish

Pour 2 1/2 c. water into large bowl with brown rice, millet and amaranth. Put bowl in steamer; steam over medium flame for 1 hour. Then mix in the rest of the ingredients while still hot.

DELICIOUS BROWN SWEET RICE

1 c. brown sweet rice or brown rice
5 - 10 Chinese mushrooms, soaked and sliced
3 ears black fungus, soaked and sliced
1/2 c. bite-sized cubes of carrot and daikon
1 T. grated ginger
1-2 T. oil
1 T. soy sauce (optional)
1/2 c. green peas
cilantro for garnish

Saute Chinese mushrooms and black fungus with a little bit of oil for 10 minutes over low flame. Turn heat off and add carrots, daikon, ginger, oil and rice, mixing well.

Put this mixture in a bowl with 1 1/3 c. water if you use sweet brown rice or 1 3/4 c. water if you use brown rice (Chinese mushroom soak water is good to use) and steam for 1 hour over medium flame.

Mix in peas, cilantro and soy sauce (or a pinch of salt) when rice is done and still hot. Garnish with cilantro.

CURRIED TAMALE

Serves 4 - 6

1/4 lb. plain tofu, mashed
1/4 c. cornmeal
2 ears fresh corn, cut off cob (choose ears with a lot of
    husks)
1/2 c. couscous
1/2 avocado, mashed
1 t. curry powder
pinch of salt

Garnish:
    toasted sesame oil
    little bit of finely chopped cilantro
      OR
    catsup

Remove the husks from the corn leaving them as whole as possible. Mix together all the ingredients except garnish and set aside for 10 minutes.

Using 2 husks, wrap up with a few spoonsful of the corn mixture. Tie with cotton string, thread or 1/4 in. strips of husk. Steam for 1/2 hour.

When serving remove the husks and add garnish.

* You may want to pick up extra husks at your produce store.

** The best way to wrap up the tamales is to fold the ends over first, then roll up the sides and tie. You can make "strings" from the corn husks about 1/4" wide.

CHARLIE'S FAVORITE PORRIDGE

Serves 4 - 6

1 c. brown rice
1/2 c. mung beans
1 carrot, sliced
2 celery stalks, chopped
1 T. dried onion
1 small piece wakame seaweed
1 t. coriander seed powder
5 Chinese mushrooms, sliced or left whole

Combine all ingredients and cook in a crockpot with 5-6 c. water for 6-8 hours, or on the stove over medium flame for 2-3 hours. When done season to taste with tamari soy sauce or Bragg's Liquid Aminos.

RICE AND PEANUTS

1 c. sweet brown rice
1 c. brown rice
1 c. peanuts, presoaked for softer ones

Steam all ingredients with 5 c. water for 1 1/2 hours, or cook
in a slow cooker for 5-6 hours.

The 2:1 grain: legume ratio is a balanced proportion for a
complete protein.

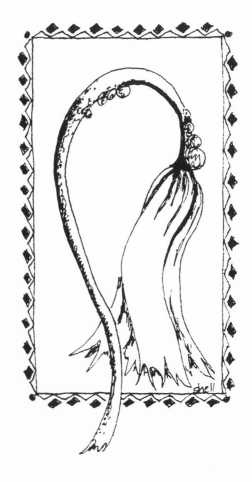

MILLET CROQUETTES

Serves 4

1 c. millet
3 scallions, finely chopped
1 small carrot, finely grated
1/2 t. basil
1 T. tamari

Cook millet with 3 c. water for 30 - 40 minutes, or until water is absorbed.

Add the rest of the ingredients and mix well. Make small balls and flatten to 2 inch wide patties on an oiled cookie sheet. Bake at 325 degrees for 20 - 30 minutes.

They should be crisp on the outside and soft inside when done.

KICHAREE

Serves 4 - 6

Kicheree literally translates as "rice and lentils" and can be used as a 3 - 10 day therapeutic fast for emotional problems, weight loss and recovery from illness. Kicharee provides easily assimilable and well balanced protein. In the summer or for heat conditions use mung beans and rice. In the winter or for cold problems use brown or red lentils and rice.

1 c. rice, white or brown
1/2 c. mung beans or lentils, soaked a few hours
2 t.- 2 T. ghee (clarified butter) or sesame oil
1 small piece wakame seaweed
1 t. turmeric powder
1 1/2 t. coriander seed powder
1/4 t. cumin seed powder
1 T. Bragg's Liquid Aminos

Combine all ingredients with at least 5 c. water and cook about 2 hours on the stove or 6-8 hours in a crockpot. More water and more cooking time will make the kicharee even easier to digest.

*For weight loss, limit diet to 3 bowls of kicharee per day, for a short period of time.

RICE PORRIDGE (CONGEE)

Congees are very easy to digest and beneficial for those recovering from illness. Vegetables or herbs can be added for therapeutic purposes.

1 c. rice
5 - 10 c. water

Cook rice for at least 2 hours or up to 8 (very low flame). This can be made in a crock pot over night.

When done choose optional garnish:
1. roasted peanuts and cilantro, finely chopped
2. green onion or chives, finely chopped
3. toasted sesame seeds

*Therapeutic additions, added at beginning of cooking:
1. 1/4 c. mung beans for heat conditions
2. 2 chopped stalks celery for insomnia, hypertension
3. 1 chopped carrot to benefit lungs and digestion
4. 1/4 c. aduki beans for edema or weak kidneys
5. 1/4 c. pine nuts for dry lungs or dry stools
6. 1 small chopped leek for cold conditions
7. 1 t. fennel seeds for gas or hernia pain.

HERB CEREALS AND DISHES

SUMMER PORRIDGE WITH HERBS

Serves 3-4

1/2 c. mung beans
1/4 c. brown rice or sweet rice
1/4 c. Job's tears (Yi Yi Ren,薏米)
1/2 c. lily bulbs (Bai He,百合), soaked in 1 c. water
1 handful Mint (Bo He,薄荷), tied in a cotton bag
honey or molassas for sweetening

In a non-metal pan add 4 c. water to the mung beans, rice
and Job's tears. Cook over a low flame until soft, then add
lily bulbs with their soak water. Turn heat to medium and
cook until lily bulbs are soft. Add the mint and turn flame
to high for 5 minutes. Turn off heat, remove cotton bag,
and add sweetener.

HERB SOUP FOR DESSERT

1/2 c. lily bulbs (Bai He, 百合), soaked in 1 c. water
1/2 c. peanuts (skinless)
1/2 c. azuki bean
honey or other sweetener

In a pan add 4 c. water and bring to a boil. Add peanuts and azuki beans, turn off heat and let set for 1 hour.

Turn heat on and simmer until soft. Then add lily bulbs, turn heat to medium and cook until lily bulbs are soft (15-20 minutes).

Turn heat off and add sweetener.

TONIC HERBS DISH

Serves 4-6

1 handful (about 1 long stick) Codonopsis (Dang Shen, 党参), soaked and sliced
1/2 c. lily bulbs (Bai He, 百合), soaked
2 T. lycii berries (Gou Qi Zi, 杞子), soaked
1 handful lily flowers, soaked
1 handful lotus root, cut into matchsticks
1 small gobo root, sliced thinly
1 piece wheat gluten or tofu cake, cut into matchsticks
1 small green pepper, cut into matchsticks
few thin slices ginger
pinch of salt

Saute all ingredients except the green pepper in a little oil or some of the herb soak water until everything is tender. Then add green pepper and a pinch of salt.

SWEET HERB PORRIDGE

3 T. Poria powder (Fu Ling,茯苓)
1 T. apricot kernel powder (Nan Xing Ren,南杏)
3 T. sesame seed meal
1 handful longan (Long Yan Rou,桂圓), diced
1 handful red dates (Da Zao, 紅棗), diced
pinch of cinnamon (Rou Gui,肉桂)

2/3 c. brown rice
2/3 c. brown sweet rice
2/3 c. barley flakes

Combine the above ingredients with at least 3 1/2 c. water
(more water for thinner porridge) and steam 1 1/2 hour.
Serve plain or topped with almond or soy milk.

EIGHT TREASURES CEREAL

Serves 5-6

1/3 c. azuki beans
1/3 c. skinless peanuts
1/3 c. lotus seeds (Lian Zi, 蓮子)
1/3 Job's tears (Yi Yi Ren, 薏米)
10 chestnuts (good for the spleen)
10 Chinese red dates (Da Zao, 紅棗)
1/3 c. dried longnans fruit (Long Yan Rou, 桂圓) or
  raisins
handful of lily bulbs (Bai He, 百合)
1 c. brown sweet rice or brown rice
millet (optional)

Bring 10 c. water to a boil. Add the first 6 ingredients; turn off the heat, cover for 1/2 hour. Turn heat on and simmer for 1/2 hour. Then put in the rice and lily bulbs and simmer for 1 hour. During the last 10 minutes of cooking, add the longnans or raisins.

* If cooked with 8 c. of water it has a drier texture. It is delicious to warm up left overs mixed with soy milk and a pinch of cinnamon for breakfast.

THE DISH RICH IN IRON

Serves 5 - 6

1/2 lb. gobo (burdock) roots, cleaned well with a brush
    then thinly sliced
1/2 lb. lotus roots
1 small carrot, thinly sliced
5 - 6 Chinese mushrooms, soaked and sliced or white
    mushrooms, sliced
1 firm tofu cake, sliced
few slices ginger
1 T. soy sauce
1 T. oil
cilantro for garnish

Saute gobo root, lotus roots and Chinese mushrooms in a
little mushroom soak water. Cook until soft, then add
carrot and cook a few minutes. Turn heat to high and add
tofu cake, ginger, soy sauce, oil and white mushrooms (if
you are using white ones).

Mix well. Turn off heat and garnish with cilantro.

GOBO BURGERS

Serves 6 - 8

3 small or 1 long gobo (burdock) root, finely grated
2 small or 1 medium carrot, finely grated
ginger, finely grated
1/4 lb. plain tofu
3 - 4 fresh water chestnuts, finely chopped (optional)
cilantro
2 T. mushroom powder
1 c. oat bran or 1/2 c. wheat flour
4 eggs
a little soy sauce or mustard stem pickle, finely chopped
sesame oil

Combine the above ingredients then fry in a small amount
of oil with the pan covered (fry both sides). This makes
about 10 burgers.

*These can also be prepared by steaming for 20 minutes.

SIX SPICE SEAWEED SILK

1 handful star anise
3/4 handful fennel seeds
small piece cinnamon
5 or 6 cloves (too many makes it bitter)
small amount pepper (black, white or Sezchuan), to taste
1/4 handful licorice

Kombu, soaked and cleaned
Ginger, sliced
Soy sauce or Chinese miso
Sesame oil

Combine spices and 5-6 c. water; cook over low flame for 30 minutes. Strain off liquid (herbs can be reused). Add to the liquid the kombu, ginger, oil, and soy sauce or miso. Cook until the kombu becomes tender. After cooking, slice kombu very thinly like strands of silk. Serve as a side dish or add to other dishes.

* Instead of making "spice tea", you can put spices in a cloth bag and cook with the kombu. Or, powder the herbs and add 2-3 T. powder to the kombu.

SWEET BREAKFAST PORRIDGE

Serves 4

3/4 c. brown rice
1/4 c. barley flakes
1/2 c. raw skinless peanuts
10 Chinese red dates (Da Zao, 紅棗)
1 slice fresh ginger

Cook all ingredients with 5 c. water in a crockpot over night or on the stove 2-3 hours. When done sweeten to taste with rice or maple syrup.

TOFU, TEMPEH AND GLUTEN DISHES

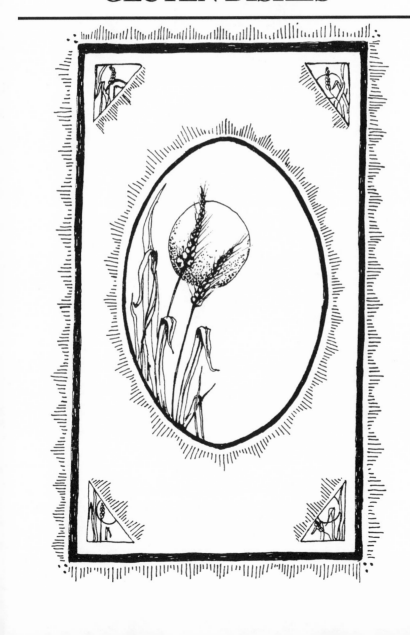

DELICIOUS GLUTEN AND GREEN VEGETABLES

Serves 6 - 8

GLUTEN:
2 c. gluten flour
5 - 10 Chinese mushrooms, soaked and finely chopped
 (or use dry and blend to powder)
1 c. jicama or carrot, finely grated
2 T. toasted sesame oil
2 T. soy sauce
1 T. ginger, finely grated
1 sheet nori, torn into small pieces

Optional:
1 t. white pepper
1 egg (if used, reduce amount of jicama)
1 square baked tofu, finely grated

Mix the above ingredients well, except the gluten flour, then mix in the gluten flour. Press into an 8" loaf pan or bowl or deep plate that will fit into your steamer. Steam over a medium flame for 1 hour. Remove from steamer, let cool then slice.

GREEN VEGETABLES:
broccoli, spinach, watercress, bok choy, Chinese peas, green beans, brussel sprouts (discard tough bottoms, then cross cut them without cutting all the way through), green leafy vegetables, etc.

Choose either two vegetables or small amounts of each. Steam over a high flame for a few minutes (brussel sprouts take a little longer).

In a large bowl combine small amounts of grated ginger, soy sauce (or miso) and oil. Add the steamed vegetables (draining off any excess water) and let them absorb the seasoning while they are still hot.

Place sliced gluten in the middle of plate then arrange the green vegetables around it.

* A dressing can be used instead of the ginger, soy sauce and oil mixture for seasoning the steamed vegetables.

** You can use Chinese mushroom soak water for the liquid used in making the gluten (1 c. liquid), instead of the jicama. This makes delicious gluten.

WHITE IN THE RED

Serves 4 - 6

1 bunch red chard
1/2 lb. white tofu, cut in bite size cubes
1 T. ginger, finely grated
1 - 2 T. oil
1 - 2 T. wheat flour or cornstarch or arrowroot, dissolved
   in a little water
pinch of salt or a little soy sauce (optional)

Clean the chard well, then separate the stems and the leaves. Cut into large pieces. Put the stems in a saucepan with a little bit of water and cook until soft over a medium flame.

Then add leaves and tofu, cover, and cook over a high flame for a few minutes until leaves get soft. If water dries out you may have to add more.

Next pour cornstarch mixture in, turn heat to medium and stir well (be gentle in stirring so you do not crumble the tofu cubes). Add grated ginger, pinch of salt, and oil; turn heat off. Serve warm.

HAIR SEAWEED GLUTEN LOAF

Serves 5-6

1 c. grated jicama
1/4 c. Chinese mushroom powder
1 t. grated ginger
1/2 c. soaked hair seaweed, chopped
1 T. soy sauce
1 T. sesame oil
1 1/2 - 2 c. gluten flour

Mix together well the first 6 ingredients. Then add the flour, a little at a time, and knead. When well mixed, press into a loaf pan and steamed for 1 hour.

The loaf can be sliced and served plain or with a gravy and cilantro garnish or cut into cubes and put into stir fried vegetables or soups.

TWO MINUTES TOFU DISH

Serves 2-4

1 lb. plain tofu

SEASONING:
1 sheet nori, torn into little pieces
sesame oil or other oil
soy sauce
one of the following herb combinations:
1. finely chopped cilantro
   grated ginger
2. finely chopped basil
   grated ginger
3. finely chopped mint
   grated ginger
4. finely chopped celery
   grated ginger

Cook whole squares of tofu in boiling water for 2 minutes
(or steam). Then put on a plate and press out some of the
water. Use a chopstick to make several holes through top
of tofu (top to bottom).

Mix together well one of the herb combinations, soy sauce
and oil, then pour over the tofu. Spread pieces of nori on
top.

PROTEIN MEDLEY

Serves 5-6

5 - 10 Chinese mushrooms, soaked and quartered
1 package tempeh, cut into 1" slices
2 bean curd sticks, soaked and cut into 2" pieces
5 inch piece kombu, cut into 1" squares
handful of Chinese peas or asparagus (2" pieces) or green
pepper (1" squares)
1 small, thin carrot, sliced
1/2 small jicama, cut into 1" squares
ginger, cut into thin strips
oil
soy sauce or a pinch of salt

Simmer Chinese mushrooms, seaweed, tempeh and bean
curd sticks in a little of the mushroom soaking water until
soft. Add carrots and cook 2 minutes, then add the rest of
the ingredients and cook a few minutes over a high flame.

STUFFED RED AND GREEN PEPPERS

Serves 6-8

3 very small red and 3 very small green pepper, cut in half with seeds and stems removed

FILLING:
1 lb. plain tofu
1/2 c. couscous or 1/2 c. wheat germ
1/4 c. Chinese mushroom powder (grind in a blender)
a little finely chopped red and green pepper

GRAVY:
3/4 - 1 c. water
1 T. preserved black soybeans or soy sauce
1 t. grated ginger
1 t. curry powder (optional)
1 T. cornstarch or other thickener
a few drops of sesame oil
cilantro for garnish

Mash tofu and add mushroom powder; mix well then cook over a high flame for 2 minutes. When hot add couscous or wheat germ and stir well. Turn off heat and set aside for 10 minutes. Divide filling into 2 parts: into one part mix finely chopped red pepper and stuff it into a green pepper; into the other part, mix finely chopped green pepper and stuff it into a red pepper.

Fry stuffed peppers in a little oil for 1 minute, then add a little bit of water, cover and cook for a few minutes. Turn off heat and place the 12 stuffed peppers on a plate.

Then prepare the gravy as follows and pour over peppers:

Bring 3/4 c. water to a boil, add preserved black beans or soy sauce, thickening and ginger. Heat and stir until thick. Add oil and stir in well.

Garnish the top with cilantro.

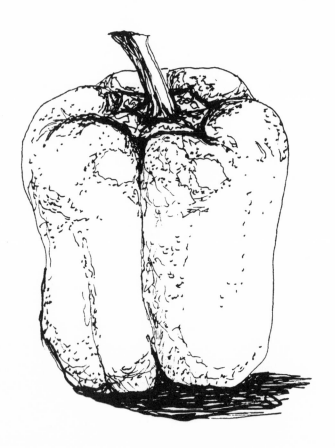

DELICIOUS MISO TEMPEH

Serves 6 - 8

1 handful green beans, cut in half
1 small carrot, halved lengthwise and then cut diagonally
1 small Italian squash, halved lengthwise and then cut
   diagonally
1 package tempeh (any kind), cut in half to a thickness of
   about 1/4" then cut into 1" squares
5 - 10 Chinese mushrooms, soaked and quartered
1 - 2 ears black fungus, soaked and cut into bite
   size pieces the same size as the mushrooms
1 - 2 T. miso
1 - 2 T. oil
1 T. cornstarch, arrowroot or other thickener
a little ginger, thin sliced
cilantro for garnish

Bring 1 c. water to a boil and add the green beans for a few
minutes. Then add carrots and cook until both are almost
tender. Next add the squash, turn heat to low and cook for
a few minutes. Remove vegetables from the water and put
them on a deep plate.

In the same pan, add a small amount of the mushroom soak
water and saute the tempeh, black fungus and Chinese
mushrooms until tender. You may need to add more
mushroom soak water if the tempeh absorbs alot of it. Add
ginger, oil and miso mixture (miso, thickener and a little
water). Stir well, then pour over the top of the vegetables.
Garnish with cilantro.

CHINESE MUSHROOMS, PEANUTS AND MISO

Serves 5 - 6

1/2-1 c. peanuts (soaked in 1 - 1 1/2 c. water overnight or
   in hot water for a few hours)
2 pieces baked tofu cake, cut into bite-size cubes
5-10 Chinese mushrooms, soaked and chopped
1/2 small red pepper, cut into bite-size cubes
a few Chinese peas, chopped
a little celery, finely chopped
toasted sesame oil, a few drops
1 T. miso or Chinese miso
1 T. finely chopped ginger, white pepper or chili pepper (if
   you want it spicy)

Cook peanuts together with soaking water for half an hour
over a low flame (turn to low after it begins to boil). Add
mushrooms and some of the soaking water and cook for
another 20 minutes, or until the peanuts get soft. Then add
the rest of the ingredients, except the oil, and turn to high
heat for a few minutes (until peas turn very green and
crisp). Stir well, turn off heat and garnish with sesame oil.

* For faster cooking, cook peanuts in a pressure cooker for
20 minutes.

CURRIED TOFU STIR FRY WITH TENDER SEAWEED

Serves 4

1 lb. plain tofu, cut into bite-sized cubes
small amount wakame seaweed (or any tender kind), soaked and chopped
1 small tomato, cut into bite-sized cubes
1/3 c. green peas
1 T. curry
1 T. thickener (cornstarch, arrowroot, etc.)
a little oil

Stir fry the tofu and curry over low flame for 5 minutes. Then add seaweed and tomato for a few minutes. Stir in thickening (dissolved in a little water) and stir well. Add peas. Turn off heat, mix in oil and stir well.

HAPPY REUNION

Serves 5-6

1/2 lb. tempeh, cut into squares or triangles
1/2 lb. tofu, cut the same
10-20 Chinese mushrooms, stems removed then soaked
1 medium carrot
1 medium daikon, peeled
1 long strip kombu, soaked and cleaned (or use hiziki)
1 can baby corn
1 bunch cilantro for garnish
1/2 c. soy sauce
5-10 slices ginger
1/8-1/4 c. oil

Pour soy sauce and 1 1/2 c. Chinese mushroom soak water into a pan; add oil, ginger, Chinese mushrooms (whole), tempeh, and tofu. Saute until mushrooms get tender (about 1/2 hour over low flame). Remove from heat and arrange attractively on a plate.

In the same pan, saute the kombu, whole daikon and whole carrot, adding more water if there is not enough cooking liquid left. (If hiziki seaweed is used instead of kombu, add it the last 5 minutes of cooking.) When a fork easily inserts into the kombu and the daikon, this mixture is done. Turn off heat, remove from pan and slice when cooled.

Garnishing the edge of the plate with cilantro.

VEGETARIAN MEAT DISH

Serves 5-6

VEGETARIAN MEAT:
1 c. gluten flour
1/2 c. grated jicama
1 t. oil
1 t. soy sauce
1 t. ginger, grated
1 sheet nori seaweed, torn into little pieces (optional)

VEGETABLES:
5-10 Chinese mushrooms, soaked and sliced
small broccoli
2 leaves red and green cabbage, cut into chunks
1 small carrot, sliced thin
few ginger slices
1 T. oil
pinch of salt

Mix vegetarian meat ingredients. Knead a little bit, then put in a bowl and steam over high flame for 30 minutes. Remove from steamer, set aside and let cool. Then slice or cut into bite size cubes

Saute sliced gluten and Chinese mushrooms in a little bit of water until tender (about 20 minutes over low flame). Turn heat to high, add vegetables, cover and cook a few minutes until done. Turn heat off and add oil and salt.

VEGETARIAN HIGH PROTEIN DISH

Serves 4 - 6

PREPARING THE GLUTEN:
1 egg
1/2 c. gluten flour
2 T. Chinese mushroom powder
2 T. soy sauce
1 T. sesame oil
2 T. water
a little ginger
a little white pepper

Mix liquid ingredients together well, then add the flour and mushroom powder and mix well. Spread out this gluten on the cutting board and cut into small pieces. Drop pieces into boiling mushroom soak water and cook for 1/2 hour over medium heat.

PREPARING THE DISH:
10 Chinese mushrooms, soaked and quartered
1/2 lb. tofu, cubed
1 package tempeh, cubed
soy sauce and grated ginger
gluten pieces from above
1 carrot, sliced
1 broccoli stalk, chopped
1 celery stalk, sliced
1 zucchini, sliced
1/2 jicama, cut into large matchsticks

Cook the tofu for a few minutes in a skillet to get rid of some of the water, then remove from pan. Cook mushrooms and tempeh together, then add the gluten, soy sauce, and some mushroom soak water.

When the tempeh is almost done, add the vegetables, carrots and broccoli first. If it dries out, add more mushroom soaking water. When everything is done, add the previously cooked tofu, grated ginger
and soy sauce. Cook a few minutes.

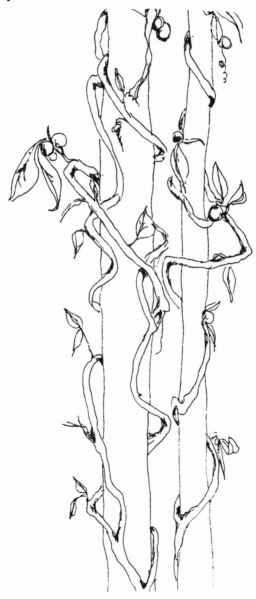

SWEET AND SOUR TOFU

1 lb. plain tofu, cut into bite size cubes
2 - 3 T. molasses or other sweetener except honey
1/2 c. ketchup
1 T. grated ginger
1 t. curry powder
2 T. cornstarch or wheat flour, dissolved in a little water
cilantro and toasted sesame oil for garnish

Fry tofu in a little oil, turning gently so as not to mash. Add molasses, ketchup, ginger and curry powder and simmer a few minutes. Add cornstarch mixture, stir well until thickened, then turn off heat and add garnish.

*Note: Honey should not be combined with tofu or soy bean milk because it becomes difficult to digest.

EGG DISHES

FRESH SPINACH EGG NOODLES

Serves 5 - 6

1 bunch fresh spinach (leaves only - save stems for soup)
4 - 5 c. whole wheat flour
1 egg

Seasoning mixture:
1/2 handful hiziki seaweed, soaked in boiling water for 1
    minute then strained
1 handful finely grated carrots
a little bit of finely chopped cilantro or parsley
1 T. finely grated ginger
1 T. oil
1 T. soy sauce

Mix together the seasoning ingredients and set aside in a
container. Clean spinach leaves well then chop into little
pieces. Blend, a little at a time, into a thick liquid. If it is
too thick for the blender, add a little water.

Mix spinach juice with egg and flour and knead like bread
dough (the longer you knead it the better it will taste).
Then use a wooden rolling pin to roll out flat (about 1/8
inch thick) and cut into 1/2 inch wide stips. Spread some
flour over the noodles to prevent sticking together.

Bring water to a boil and add the fresh noodles, using a
chopstick to stir and avoid them sticking together. When
the water is boiling again, strain off the water and add into
the seasoning mixture. Mix well.

SCRAMBLED EGG TOFU

Serves 6

1 lb. white tofu, mashed
3 eggs, beaten
2 T. cornstarch, or other thickener
1 T. soy sauce or miso

Garnish:
2 T. finely grated carrot
1 T. miso, dissolved in a little water
cilantro, finely chopped
toasted sesame oil

Scramble the tofu and egg mixture until done. Pour onto a dish and garnish the top with the carrot, cilantro, miso and a few drops of sesame oil.

SIX SPICE EGGS AND MORE

12 peeled hard boiled eggs (add a pinch of salt while
   boiling for easier peeling)
5 slices ginger
1/3 c. soy sauce
2 T. oil

Combine the above ingredients in a pan with 2 c. water.
Add the following spices which have been placed in a small
cotton bag (then removed when ready):
1 T. cinnamon
1 T. cloves
1 T. fennel
1 t. pepper
1/2 handful star anise
1/2 handful licorice
Simmer about 1/2 hour until eggs turn a deep brown color.
Turn the eggs over during the cooking so that they will be
evenly colored.

After cooking the eggs, you can use the spice liquid to cook
tofu, tempeh, seaweed, black fungus and more.

WATERCRESS EGGS

Serves 2

1/2 bunch watercress, cleaned and
  chopped
2 eggs
1/2 handful hiziki seaweed, soaked
  and chopped
1 t. soy sauce
1 t. oil

Mix ingredients well then fry in a
little bit of oil.

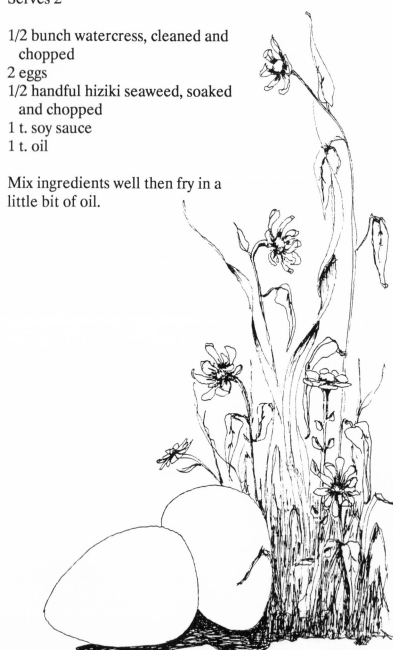

TARO ROOT CAKE

1 lb. taro roots, peeled and finely grated
  (large ones taste the best)
2 eggs
3-4 Chinese mushrooms, finely chopped
1/4 c. carrots, finely chopped
1/4 c. daikon, finely chopped
a little soy sauce and oil, to taste
a little cilantro and ginger, finely chopped

Saute Chinese mushrooms, carrots and daikon in a little oil for a few minutes. Turn heat off and mix in the rest of the ingredients. Mix well then pour into a loaf pan and steam over medium flame for 40 minutes.

MUSHROOM BURGERS WITH BABY CORN AND ASPARAGUS

1-2 handfuls Chinese mushroom stems, separated from
   tops when dry and soaked and finely chopped
1 egg
2 T. flour
1 t." 5 Spice Powder" (optional)
1/4 t. white pepper (optional)
sesame oil
soy sauce
grated ginger

Beat egg, mix with other ingredients. Form patties and fry
in a little oil on both sides. Decorate plate with steamed
baby corn and asparagus.

* These burgers can also be put on a wheat bun and eaten
like a hamburger with catsup, pickle, etc.

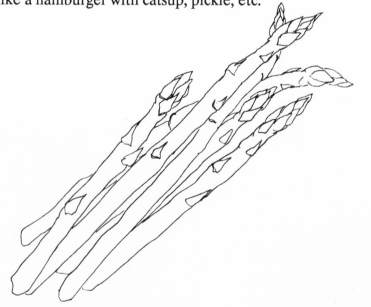

SPINACH PANCAKE

1 handful chopped spinach
2 T. whole wheat flour
1 egg
few drops toasted sesame oil
little bit of soy sauce
little bit of grated ginger
1 sheet nori seaweed, torn into small pieces

Mix together all ingredients and fry on both sides in a pancake shape.

*This is a very nutritious and delicious pancake. The spinach provides iron and the nori is rich in calcium and other minerals. It is also good for those on a reducing diet.

SWEET AND SOUR EGGS

Serves 2-3

3 - 4 eggs, beaten
1 - 2 T. ketchup
2 T. honey
cilantro and toasted sesame oil for garnish

Scramble eggs in small amount of oil. When done turn off heat and mix with honey and ketchup. Garnish with cilantro and toasted sesame oil.

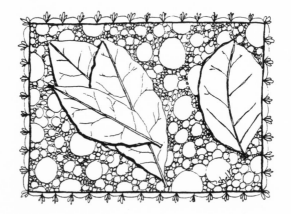

TOFU, LIMA BEAN AND EGG DISH

Serves 4 - 5

1/2 package frozen lima beans, defrosted
1/2 lb. plain tofu, cut into bite size cubes
2 eggs, beaten
1 handful brocolli tops
1 T. grated ginger
little bit of grated carrot for garnish

Cook tofu and lima beans in a little bit of water over medium flame until the lima beans get soft (about 5 minutes). Turn heat to high, add brocolli and cook until done, leaving it crisp. Put into a bowl without the liquid.

Scramble eggs and ginger in a little oil. When done turn heat off and stir in the lima bean, tofu and brocolli mixture. Add a pinch of salt and garnish with grated carrot.

*Note: Use the large size lima beans if possible because they are much creamier than the baby lima beans.

VEGETABLE DISHES

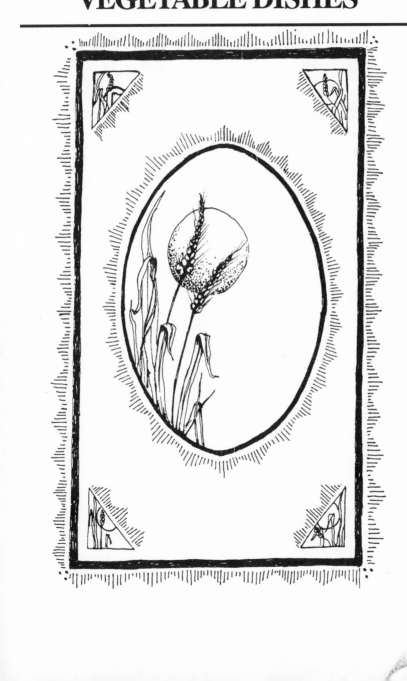

SPRING COMES

Serves 5 - 6

1 basket brussel sprouts
1 lb. plain tofu (in water)
few slices ginger
pinch of salt or a little miso

Garnish:
small amount chopped red pepper
small amount chopped cilantro
small amount cubed avocado

Clean the brussel sprouts well and discard the tough stems, then make a cross cut on the bottoms.
Steam over high flame until soft. Pour off the water that may have come out, and place brussel sprouts on a plate.

Steam tofu until warm (2 - 3) minutes, then put tofu, ginger and a pinch of salt (or miso) into the blender and blend well. Pour over the brussel sprouts and garnish the top with red pepper, cilantro and avocado.

CREAMY AND RICH CORN DISH

Serves 4 - 5

1/3 c. skinless peanuts (soaked in 3 c. water)
2 ears fresh corn (cut corn off cobs)
1/3 c. each, cut into tiny cubes:
carrots
jicama
potato
1 small tomato, cubed
cilantro for garnish
a few drops of sesame oil

Bring peanuts to a boil, turn to low and simmer until soft
(about 40 minutes). Add corn, carrots, jicama, and potato.
Simmer until soft. Add tomato and turn flame to high for
2 minutes. Then turn off heat; garnish with cilantro and a
few drops of sesame oil.

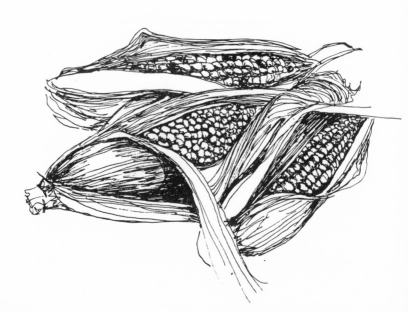

STEAMED WHITE BLOSSOM

Serves 5 or 6

1 medium cauliflower
2-3 Chinese mushrooms, soaked and sliced
1 can or 1 bag fresh golden needle (enoki) mushrooms
  or 1/2 lb. white mushrooms
1/2 small red pepper, sliced
1 - 2 small ears black fungus, soaked and sliced
1/2 handful jicama matchsticks
1/2 handful hiziki, soaked (optional)
1 T. oil
1 T. soy sauce
1-2 T. thickener, dissolved in a little water
a few very thin matchsticks of ginger
a few drops of toasted sesame oil

Cut off leaves and a little bit of stem from the cauliflower.
Leave the cauliflower whole, wash well then steam the
whole flower until soft enough for a toothpick to go
through the center (be sure not to cook too soft). This will
take about 10 - 15 minutes over a high flame. When done
remove from steamer, place on a large plate and set aside
to cool. Cut into 6 pieces (like a cake) leaving the
cauliflower all together (not separating the pieces yet).

While the cauliflower is cooling, prepare the following.
Saute Chinese mushrooms and black fungus using the
mushroom soak water, until they get soft. Add golden
mushrooms, red pepper, jicama, hiziki and ginger and cook
1-2 minutes.

Add thickener, mix and stir well. Turn off heat, add soy
sauce and oil and mix well, then pour over the cauliflower.
Garnish with cilantro.

SEAWEED AND VEGETABLE TEMPURA

Serves 5-10

1/2 handful hiziki, soaked 20 minutes, or in hot water for
  5 minutes (or substitute torn pieces of nori)
1 handful green beans, cut in half
1 small carrot, cut diagonally to match size of green beans
1 small gobo root, cut diagonally like carrots
4-5 Chinese mushrooms, soaked, cleaned and sliced

Batter:
1-2 c. flour
1 egg
1/2 t. white pepper
1 T. miso
a little grated ginger
a little chopped cilantro
a little curry powder (optional)
few drops toasted sesame oil
a little water

Mix the batter well. Dip small amounts of vegetable and
seaweed in batter and fry in hot oil over medium flame on
both sides. To keep vegetables crisp, do not over fry.

VARIATION:
2-3 medium Italian squashes, cut into chunks with small
amount of miso spread on each piece before dipping into
batter, then fried as above.

NAPA ROLLS

1 long strip kombu, soaked and cleaned
1 large head of Napa cabbage, washed and leaves
   separated whole
1 package tofu cake, sliced into 1/2" sticks

toothpicks to fasten

Cook the whole strip of kombu with 2 c. water and one of
the following:
   1. 1/2 handful star anise, few slices ginger, 1/4 t.toasted
      sesame oil and 1/2 c. soy sauce
   2. a few slices ginger, toasted sesame oil and 1/2 c. soy
      sauce

When the kombu is soft enough that a toothpick can easily
go through it, remove from pan and allow it to cool.

Steam cabbage until soft. Set aside.

Lay down one cabbage leaf, followed by a piece of kombu
(about 2-2 1/2" square), then tofu cake stick. Roll up and
fasten with a toothpick.

SWEET AND SOUR CABBAGE

1/2 head of green cabbage, chopped finely
1/2 c. tart apple juice
grated ginger
2 T. arrowroot, cornstarch or other thickener
soy sauce to taste

Cook cabbage until done in a little bit of water. Combine apple juice, ginger and thickener and add to hot cabbage, stirring over flame until thick. Season to taste with soy sauce.

VARIATION:
Instead of apple juice, combine the juice of 1 lemon, 2 t. honey and 1/2 c. of water

COOLING DISH FOR A HOT SUMMER DAY

Serves 6

1 medium brocolli, cut into bite size pieces
1 medium carrot, cut into bite size pieces

Topping:
1 lb. white tofu, excess water removed
1-2 T. miso
1 T. ginger, grated
a little oil
cilantro, chopped for garnish

Steam or cook brocolli and carrots, being sure not to over cook brocolli. Put on a plate and set aside.

Steam tofu for 2 - 3 minutes, then blend the topping ingredients at high speed, using a wooden spoon to help mix well, then pour over cooked vegetables. Garnish with cilantro.

MIXED VEGETABLE PIE

Crust:
3/4 c. unbleached white flour
1/4 c. whole wheat pastry flour
1/2 stick butter
cold water

Filling:
4 eggs
4 c. lightly sauteed vegetables (a combination of carrots,
   brocolli, squash, brussel sprouts, mushrooms, etc.)

Combine flours, then add butter with a fork until well mixed. Add enough cold water to hold dough together. Roll out the crust on a floured board and put into pie plate; pre-bake for 10 minutes at 375 degrees.

Fill crust with cooked vegetable and pour beaten eggs over the top. Bake 30 minutes at 375 degrees.

VARIATION:
Top with grated cheese or soy cheese the last 10 minutes of baking.

SESAME CARROTS WITH NORI

2 carrots, sliced
1 sheet nori, torn in small pieces
4 oz. thin noodles, cooked and drained
2 scallions, chopped finely
1 sprig basil, chopped finely
cilantro for garnish

Saute carrots in a little sesame oil, ghee or Chinese mushroom soak water. When almost soft add scallions, nori and basil and cook for about a minute. Stir in the cooked noodles and sesame seeds. Season to taste with a little soy sauce or Bragg's Liquid Aminos. If you did not cook in oil, add a few drops of toasted sesame oil before serving. Garnish with cilantro.

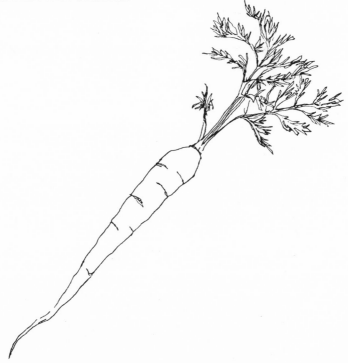

LO HAN JIA (MONK'S FARE)

Serves 4 - 6

When travelling in China, vegetarian food is sometimes difficult to order. This is what you want to ask for to get some variation of a vegetarian dish fit for a monk.

2 carrots, diagonally sliced
10 Chinese mushrooms, soaked and sliced (save the
      soaking water for cooking)
1 burdock root (gobo), diagonally sliced
1 ear black fungus, soaked and sliced
1 piece wakame seaweed, soaked and sliced
2 pieces tofu cake or gluten, cubed
2-4 other seasonal vegetables, cut or cubed such as squash,
      cabbage, bell pepper, brocolli, etc.
1 T. salted black beans (or more - season to taste)
toasted sesame oil (season to taste)
cilantro for garnish

Cook the mushrooms, carrots, burdock, black fungus and any other slow cooking vegetables in a little mushroom soak water. You may need to add more soak water as it dries out.

When these vegetables are almost soft add the wakame, tofu, salted black beans and faster cooking vegetables (i.e. squash, brocolli, cabbage, etc.)

When these are done stir in the sesame oil. Turn off flame and garnish with cilantro.

DESSERTS AND SWEET TREATS

YEAST-FREE APPLE BREAD

DOUGH INGREDIENTS:
3 c. whole wheat flour or 2 c. whole wheat flour and 1 c.
  white unbleached flour
1/3 c. walnuts
1/3 c. raisins

APPLE PASTE INGREDIENTS:
3 medium apples, peeled and finely grated
1/4 - 1/2 c. whole wheat or white flour (or barley flour)

Optional:
1 banana, mashed (use only 2 apples if used)
oil, a little bit

Place 3 c. of flour in a bowl and add 1 c. water (for softer bread, add an egg or a little more water). Mix well, then knead for 2 minutes. Set aside.

While the dough sets, peel and grate the apples into a bowl; add oil, wheat or barley flour (and mashed banana, if used) to make a paste.

Knead the dough for a few more minutes, then add the nuts and raisins and knead evenly into the dough. Spread some flour on the cutting board, then roll the dough flat with a rolling pin to about 8 inches wide and as long and thin as you can roll it. Then spread the apple paste evenly over the surface. Roll up the dough and put into a loaf pan. Put into a steamer and steam for 1/2 hour over a high flame.

MILLET CAKE WITH TOFU
FROSTING

1 c. millet
1 c. couscous
1/3 c. raisins
1/3 c. walnuts, finely chopped
1 medium apple, cut into bite size cubes (optional)
1 T. cinnamon powder (optional)

Soak millet and couscous in 2 c. water and set aside for an hour. Add walnuts and raisins, and mix well.

Oil an 8" cake pan, then press 1/2 millet/couscous mixture into the bottom. In the middle, spread the chopped apples and cinnamon, then press the rest of the millet/couscous on the top. If apples are not used press all of the millet mixture in pan at one time.

Put into a steamer and steam for 30 - 40 minutes over a medium flame. When the millet gets soft it is done.

TOFU FROSTING:
1 lb. plain tofu, squeeze out excess water
1/4 c. or more brown rice syrup or other syrup, but not
   honey
1 T. oil

Blend above ingredients well in blender (use wooden spoon to help press down the tofu). Then spread on top of millet cake.

*This tofu frosting is delicious on any kind of cake.

STEAMED PEANUT, RICE AND GINGER CAKE

Serves 6 - 8

1/2 c. skinless peanuts
1/2 c. brown or sweet rice
1/4 c. millet
1/4 c. couscous
1/8 c. oat bran
1/2 c. raisins
1 T. ginger, grated

Soak the first five ingredients in 2 1/2 c. water overnight or in hot water for a few hours. Mix in the raisins and ginger, then press into a pie pan. Steam for 1 hour over medium flame.

BLACK SESAME, WALNUT AND APRICOT SEED CAKE

3 T. apricot kernels (Nan Xing Ren, 南 杏)
1/4 - 1/2 c. black sesame seeds
1/4 c. black beans

Soak the above three ingredients in 2 1/2 c. water then blend.

2 c. sweet rice, brown rice or whole wheat flour
1/3 - 1/2 c. walnuts, diced
1/3 - 1/2 c. raisins
dates (optional)

Combine the ingredients above and put into a pie plate or dish and steam for 1 hour.

ENERGY SNACKS

1/3 - 1/2 c. barley malt or brown rice syrup or other syrup

Choose the ingredients of one of the following types of snacks or be creative and combine what you like. Any kind of nuts can be used.

1. SEAWEED SNACKS
    cilantro, finely chopped
    1 sheet nori, torn into small pieces
    1/4 c. black sesame meal (make in blender)
    1 c. oatmeal or barley flakes
    1/2 c. oat bran
    1/4 c. walnuts, chopped finely
    1/4 c. cooked wheat berries (optional)

2. GINGER COOKIE
    1 T. grated ginger
    1/4 c. quinoa
    1 c. oatmeal or barley flakes
    1/2 c. oat bran or wheat germ
    1/4 c. raisins
    1/3 c. brown sesame seeds or meal
    1/4 c. sunflower seeds
    1/4 c. apple juice
    1/4 c. cooked wheat berries (optional)

3. VANILLA COOKIE
    2 t. vanilla
    1 T. fruit juice
    1 c. oatmeal or wheat germ
    1/2 c. oat bran
    1/4 c. walnuts
    1/4 c. almonds, chopped

1/4 c. raisins
1/4 c. cooked wheat berries (optional)

4. COCONUT SNACK
1/3 c. coconut flakes
1 c. oatmeal
1/2 c. oat bran
1/8 c. pineapple juice
1/4 c. pine nuts
1/4 c. cashews
1/4 c. raisins
1/4 c. cooked wheat berries (optional)

5. AZUKI BEAN COOKIE
1/4 c. cooked azuki beans
1 c. oatmeal
1/2 c. oat bran
1/4 c. brown sesame seeds or meal
1/4 c. raisins
1/4 c. chopped Brazil nuts
2 t. cinnamon
1/4 c. cooked wheat berries (optional)

6. CAROB COOKIE
1/3 c. carob powder or chips
1/8 c. lemon juice
1 c. oatmeal
1/2 c. oat bran
1/4 c. pecans
1/4 c. sunflower or pumpkin seeds
1/4 c. raisins (optional)
1/4 c. cooked wheat berries (optional)

Dry stir fry the oatmeal, grain flakes, grain flours or bran.
Combine all ingredients in a bowl. Cook the barley malt
in a large pan on low flame until it gets hot, then turn heat

off and add the already mixed ingredients. Mix well. Wet hands and form small balls while warm, then let cool.

* You can substitute wheat germ, soy bean powder or rice bran for the oat bran. Any dried fruits can be added for sweetness. Any grain flakes (barley, rice, millet, etc.) can be used instead of the oatmeal.

** To make a less sweet cookie, add 1 t. miso dissolved in a little water.

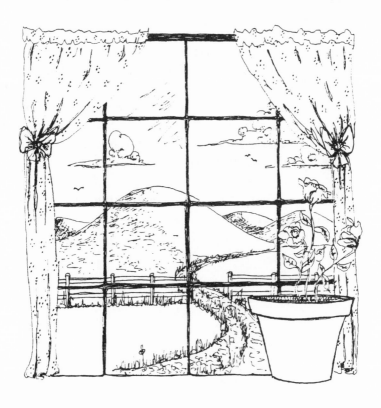

LONGAN AND WALNUT COOKIES

1/2 c. black sesame powder (make in blender)
1/2 c. chopped walnuts
1/4 c. chopped longans (Long Yan Rou, 桂圓) or raisins
1 c. oatmeal
1/2 t. miso, dissolved in 1 T. water
1/4 c. wheat germ
1/2 c. brown rice syrup

Choose one of the following methods of preparation:

1. Heat up brown rice syrup until thin, then add dissolved miso. Turn heat off and add the rest of the ingredients. Mix well then shape into balls using wet hands.

2. Dry stir fry the oatmeal and wheat germ for a few minutes. In another pan heat up the brown rice syrup until thin. Turn heat off and mix with the rest of the ingredients. Then wet hands and form into balls.

* This is a very nutritious cookie that builds blood and tonifies the kidneys and the brain.

STEAMED BANANA WALNUT CAKE

1 c. couscous soaked in 1 c. pineapple coconut juice
1 c. pineapple coconut juice blended with 2 bananas
1/2 c. coconut
1/2 c. walnuts
1/4 c. raisins
barley flour
cornmeal
lycii berries (Gou Qi Zi, 杞 子) for decoration (option-al)

Mix everything but the flours. Add enough barley flour and cornmeal to make a thick batter.

Decorated the top with lycii berries or some of the raisins and steam 45 minutes.

HEAVENLY KANTEN

1 qt. pineapple coconut juice
1/3 c. agar flakes
pinch nutmeg

Combine these and bring to a boil. Simmer about 10 minutes then add 2 T. kuzu dissolved in a little cold juice or water. Stir constantly until it comes to a boil again and is thickened.

Pour into a rectangular baking dish half filled with chopped fresh fruit such as:
  bananas
  pineapple
  mango

Then, let it "set" for 2 hours at room temperature or faster in the refrigerator. When the kanten is almost "set" add kiwi slices and mint leaves or other decorative fruits. Edible flowers make a beautiful garnish, i.e. johnny-jump-ups, violets and allysums.

*Another good combination of fruits to use is cherries, grapes, tangerines, and kiwis.

**Apple juice and cherry juice also make delicious kantens.

WHITE HERBS DESSERT FOR STRENGTHENING LUNGS

1 handful white fungus (Bai Mu Er, 白木耳), soaked and
  cleaned (remove tough bottom)
1 c. skinless peanuts
1 1/2 c. lily bulbs (Bai He, 百 合), soaked in 3 c. water
1/2 c. - 1 c. brown rice syrup or honey

In a non-metal pot, bring 5 - 6 c. water to a boil. Turn off
heat and add peanuts and white fungus; cover for 1/2 hour.

Turn heat on again and bring to a boil, then turn heat to
low and simmer until white fungus is tender (about 2
hours).

Next, add soaked lily bulbs and their soaking water, turn
heat to medium and cook until lily bulbs are tender (about
20 minutes). Add sweetener when serving.

CINNAMON APPLESAUCE

6-8 apples
2 T. honey or a small handful of raisins
1/4 t. cinnamon

Peel, core and grate apples and cook until soft (about 30 minutes). When done add cinnamon and honey. If raisins are used for sweetener, add them at the beginning of cooking apples.

To preserve for later use, put hot applesauce into sterilized mason jars, seal with sterilized lids and turn jars upside down until cool. You can tell if jars sealed by the center of the lid that should be indented. If the jar did not seal, store in refrigerator and use within a couple of weeks.

WALNUT PUDDING

2 c. soy bean milk
1/2 c. walnuts (or pecans)
1/4 - 1/3 c. maple or brown rice syrup
3 T. kuzu, arrowroot or sweet rice flour
2 T. carob powder (optional)

Blend all ingredients well. Then heat over low flame until thickened, stirring constantly.

Serve warm with a fresh mint leaf on top.

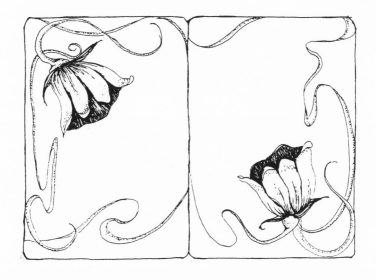

MOON CAKES (LOTUS SEED PANCAKES)

2 c. lotus seeds (Lian Zi, 蓮 子), soaked in 3 c. boiling
   water for 1 hour
1/3 - 1/2 c. honey
2 - 3 potatoes
1/2 - 1 c. whole wheat flour
1 egg
3 - 4 hard boiled egg yolks or salted duck egg yolk
   (preserved egg, hardboiled)
cold pressed oil (optional)

Cook lotus seeds over low flame until soft, then mash into
a paste. Add honey and a little oil (optional) and set aside.

Cook potatos until soft then mash. When cool, add the egg,
flour and a little oil (optional); mix well.

Divide the egg yolks into 3 or 4 pieces. Wet hands and take
1/2 handful of the potato mixture and press flat. Then put
1 T. lotus seed paste in the center, followed by a piece of
egg yolk in the middle. Cover with the potato mixture,
shaping into a flat round moon.

Fry on both sides in a non-stick pan, covered, over a low
flame.

APPENDICES

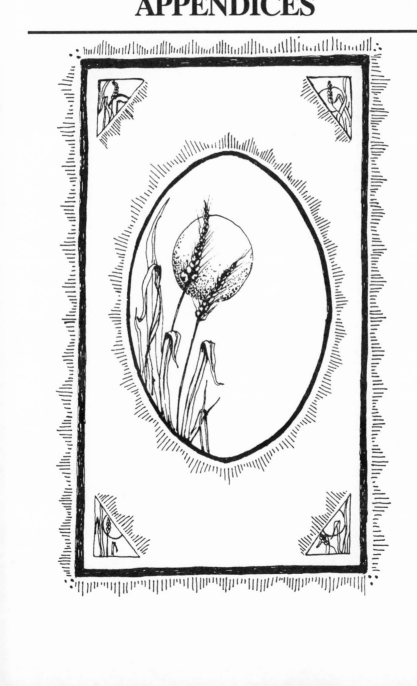

APPENDIX 1:

COOKING WITH HERBS

The age old tradition of cooking with herbs is a universal phenomena. Each culture develops its own flavor of herb usage. From India we get the spicy curries with such herbs as turmeric, coriander, cumin, red pepper, black mustard seeds and fenugreek seeds. The particular blend varies according to the locale of its derivation. From Chinese cooking we get ginger, scallions, and "Chinese 5 Spice", a blend of fennel seeds, star anise seeds, cloves, cinnamon and pepper. This blend also has many variation according to the cook. And can you imagine Italian tomato sauce without basil and oregano? Herbs are a part of cooking world-wide.

We often see that what appears as a seasoning herb is actually therapeutic. Early American settlers cooked their fowl with sage stuffing because sage preserved the meat. Hot weather countries tend toward hot, spicy herbs - have you ever wondered why? The spicy flavor is dispersive and sends our inner heat outward, thereby cooling us off. Remember the last time you ate a hot Mexican salsa that made you sweat and blow your nose.

Chinese cooking, particularly Chinese vegetarian cooking, utilizes many of the tonic (strengthening) herbs in daily cooking. A common usage is to add herbs to a grain porridge, the choice of herbs depending on physical needs. Herbs are considered "special foods" which are like powerhouses of nutrients. A partial list of those commonly used Chinese herbs follows:

CHINESE HERBS USED IN COOKING

APRICOT SEED (XING REN, 杏 仁): lubricates lungs and large intestines; stops cough. Nan Xing Ren (Southern grown) is sweet and non-toxic. Bai Xing Ren (Northern grown) is bitter and toxic in large doses. When cooking with Bai Xing Ren, remove apex. Generally, sweet ones are used in cooking.

ASTRAGALUS (HUANG QI,黄 芪): energy tonic, invigorates spleen and strengthens outer protective qi (energy); deep immune system enhancer

BLACK BEAN, PRESERVED (DAN DOU CHI, 豆 豉): relieves exterior symptoms and restlessness; benefits kidney

BLACK FUNGUS (MU ER, 黑 木 耳): cleans and strengthens the lungs; removes stagnation; nourishes stomach, calms spirit; cleanses the small and large intestines; lubricates; promotes circulation. Do not use raw and minimally when pregnant.

BLACK SESAME SEED (HU MA,黑芝麻): tonifies kidneys, moistens intestines

BURDOCK ROOT (牛蒡根): clears heat and detoxifies; cleans blood; strengthens lungs and improves skin; dispels wind; brightens vision; high in iron and other minerals. In Japanese markets it is called "gobo". Do not use with diarrhea.

CHINESE CHIVE (XIE BAI, 韮菜): warms digestion and sexual functions; anti-toxin; removes dampness. Flat in appearance; the flowers are often sold in Chinatown markets.

CHINESE FIVE SPICE (五香粉): This blend is often used for flavoring meat and tofu dishes. The herbs warm up digestion for these concentrated proteins. Put herbs in a cotton bag and cook in soups, removing at the end; or powder and sprinkle into food.
  fennel seed - 1 handful
  star anise - 1 handful
  cloves - 5 buds
  cinnamon - small piece
  pepper - 10 corns

  Optional:
   orange peel - small piece
   ginger root - small piece
   licorice - 2 slices

CHRYSANTHEMUM (JU HUA, 菊花): clears heat; soothes liver; benefits eyes, high blood pressure, and coronary heart disease

CILANTRO / CHINESE OR MEXICAN PARSLEY / CORIANDER LEAF (Yan Shi, 香菜): promotes sweating; strengthens digestion; dispels wind; promotes energy flow

CINNAMON (ROU GUI, 肉桂): strengthens stomach; warms kidney and general coldness

CODONOPSIS (DANG SHEN, 党参): tonifies energy; strengthens spleen; similar to ginseng but milder

CORDYCEPS (DONG CHONG XIA CAO, 冬虫夏草): strengthens weakness, benefits vital essence; relieves cough and dissolves phlegm; ventilates lung qi. Often cooked with ginseng in soup.

DANG GUI (當歸): tonifies and moves blood, warms inner organs; benefits irregular menses; moistens. This is traditionally cooked with chicken after childbirth or blood loss.

DIOSCOREA / CHINESE YAM (SHAN YAO, 山藥): invigorates spleen; astringent; strengthens lung and kidney; stops diarrhea

EURYALES / FOX NUT BARLEY (QIAN SHI, 芡實): tonifies spleen; consolidates kidney; nourishes heart and calms spirit

FENNEL SEED (XIAO HUI XIANG, 小茴香): unblocks and regulates flow of energy; strengthens digestion; dispels cold; stimulates peristalsis

GARLIC (DA SUAN, 大蒜): detoxifies; removes food and blood stagnation; very warming; anti-viral; anti-bacterial; detoxifies meat and seafood

GINGER (SHENG JIANG, 生薑): detoxifies; promotes sweating; warming to digestion, stops nausea

GINKO NUTS /WHITE NUTS (BAI GUO, 白菓): consolidates lung and benefits chronic cough and asthma; TOXIC RAW. This is one of the most ancient plant on the earth. The leaves are used to regenerate the brain in old age and senility.

GINSENG (REN SHEN, 人參): tonifies energy; warms body; strengthens spleen and lungs. This is a strong tonic that is contraindicated in heat conditions, infections and hypertension.

HAWTHORN BERRIES (SHAN ZHA, 山楂): benefits digestion, particularly of meats; lowers blood pressure

JOB'S TEARS / COIX (YI YI REN, 薏苡): benefits joints; clears heat; improves skin; removes dampness; tonifies lungs; invigorates spleen. Contraindicated in pregnancy.

JUJUBE DATE (DA ZAO, 大棗): strengthens spleen and stomach; nourishes blood; calms the mind

KUDZU / PUERIA ROOT (GE GEN, 葛根): soothes muscle tension; purges heat; absorbs toxins; useful in colds, stiff neck, and alcohol intoxication. This can be used as a thickening agent, similar to arrowroot.

LICORICE (GAN CAO, 甘草): detoxifies; soothes lungs and throat; tonifies spleen; "the great harmonizer" of herbs

LILY BULBS (BAI HE, 百合): lubricate lungs; nourish yin; cools the heart; calms the mind

LILY FLOWERS (金針): clears heat; anodyne; contain iron. These day lilies are easy to grow.

LONGANS (LONG YAN ROU, 桂圓): nourish heart and spleen; tonic for blood; calms the mind

LOTUS ROOT (蓮 藕): very healing; clears heat; relieves irritability; cools the blood; stops bleeding; strengthens stomach and lungs; benefits hypertension

LOTUS SEEDS (LIAN ZI, 蓮 子): tonifies spleen; astringent; strengthens kidneys; nutritive tonic

LYCII BERRIES (GOU QI ZI, 杞子): replenishes liver and kidney yin; nourishes blood; improves eyesight

OPHIOPOGONIS TUBERS (MAI MEN DONG, 麥冬): tonify yin, moisten lungs

ORANGE (TANGERINE) PEEL (CHEN PI, 陳 皮): soothes and unblocks energy; dries dampness; relieves mucus conditions

PERILLA / BEEFSTEAK LEAF (ZI SU YE, 紫苏葉): dissipates coldness; moves energy; soothes stomach; detoxifier; stops vomiting

PORIA COCOS (FU LING, 茯苓): removes dampness; strengthens spleen; calms the mind

SCALLION (CONG BAI, 葱 白): expels external pathogens; dispels wind and cold; induces sweating; anti-viral and anti-bacterial

SEAWEED (KUN BU, 昆布): promotes diuresis; softens hardenings; detoxifies; benefits glands; benefits lymphatics; alkalinizes blood; neutralizes radioactive material; contains many minerals

SHOU WU / HE SHOU WU (首 烏): Raw - lubricates intestines; purges boil-poison. Cooked - tonic for liver and kidneys; nourishes blood and sperms; strengthens bones and tendons

SHITAKE MUSHROOM / CHINESE BLACK MUSH-ROOM (香 菇): strengthens kidney and stomach; promotes healing; lowers blood pressure; anti-tumor; detoxifies; cleans intestines

SOLOMAN'S SEAL/POLYGONATI OFFICINALIS (YU ZHU, 玉竹): nourishes yin; soothes dryness

TIENCHI / PANAX NOTOGINSENG (SANCHI, 三七): Raw - disperses bruises; stops bleeding; disperses swelling; relieves shock and pain. Cooked - used for anemia and loss of blood.

WAX GOURD PEEL (DONG GUI PI, 冬瓜皮): diuretic. This makes a dark, rich broth.

WHITE FUNGUS (BAI MU ER, 白木耳): invigorates circulation; clears lung heat; strengthens digestion; promotes body fluids; lubricates; nourishes yin

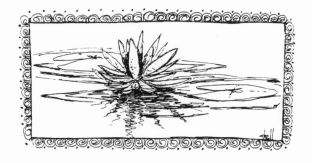

APPENDIX 2:

THE CULINARY HERB GARDEN

One of the delights in my life is growing and using cooking herbs. There's nothing like fresh basil and oregano to make that Italian dinner really special. Or garnishing that baked potato with fresh chives and dill, and serving herb butter on your rosemary rolls. Herbs enhance foods on many planes: nutritionally, visually and, of course, through tastes and smells.

Most culinary herbs grow as perennials, which in mild climates means an almost year-round supply of delicious greenery. Rosemary, sage, thyme, winter savory, oregano, mint and chives are among the more hardy; marjoram, tarragon and lovage are more delicate and die back in winter. Basil, cilantro, summer savory and dill need to be re-planted each spring. Parsley will grow for two years.

Many of the culinaries grow well in containers. My container of choice is old whiskey barrels sawed in half with holes drilled in the bottom. I have several of them right outside my kitchen door. Large clay pots and wooden window boxes are also good. Since most of the cooking herbs like plenty of sun, they will also need plenty of water, especially if grown in containers.

My favorite culinary herb is basil. Plant the seeds when the threat of frost has passed and you will enjoy basil until the weather gets really cold. Prolong the growing season by pinching back the flowers regularly. There are many interesting varieties of basil to choose from: sweet, bush, cinnamon, lemon, anise, purple and holy. Each has its slightly different personality. Basil is traditionally used to compliment tomato and vegetable dishes. I love it with tofu or eggs. In India, basil is considered a sacred plant that is grown for purification and protection.

Cilantro is a multi-cultural herb, used extensively in Mexican, Indian and Chinese dishes. The seeds of cilantro are known as coriander, one of the components of curry powder. Cilantro is very easy to grow, preferring the earth to a container, and cool spring days to hot summer ones. This lacey leaf makes a beautiful garnish on top of miso soup.

Dill's feathery leaves and tiny yellow flowers are an attractive addition to the garden; dill, like cilantro, will go to seed quickly in hot weather. The flavor is slightly tangy and goes well with light foods like cucumbers, tofu and dairy products. Summer savory is another delicious annual, used in beans and soups. It has a more pungent flavor than its hardier cousin, winter savory, which is used similarly. Savory is used to make beans more easily digestible.

If you've never gardened before, start with one of your favorite cooking herbs. Learn all about how it grows and what it likes. And remember to plant some edible flowers: nasturtiums, violets, pansies and borage are my favorites. Before long you too will be enjoying the many pleasures of your culinary herb garden.

APPENDIX 3:

ENJOYING EDIBLE FLOWERS

Flowers open up a new world of culinary pleasures. Simple summer salads become festive dishes with the addition of colorful edible blossoms for garnish. Picture a green salad topped with a rainbow of red pineapple sage, orange nasturtium, yellow fennel, purple hyssop and blue borage flowers. Most of the edible flowers are easily grown in small gardens or containers. Others can be gathered from the wilds.

Some of the most delicious flowers come from the culinary herbs. The sweet blossoms of lemon thyme, basil, cilantro and anise hyssop are a few of my favorites. Nasturtium, mustard, wild radish and chive blossoms have a delightfully pungent flavor that wakes up your taste buds. Johnny jump ups, pansies and calendula petals impart a neutral flavor and colorful flair. Borage, elder, red clover, pineapple guava, alyssum and honeysuckle are very sweet. Feverfew, yarrow, and dandelion are bitter but beautiful. Carnation petals are spicy at the tips and bitter toward the center. Ancient Romans flavored wine with carnations.

EDIBLE FLOWERS include the following:
Alkanet (Anchusa azurea or officinalis)
Anise Hyssop/ Licorice Mint (Agastache foeniculum)
Apple Blossom (Malus spp.)
Alyssum (Alyssum maritimum)
Basil (Ocimum basilicum)
Bee Balm (Monarda didyma)

Borage (Borago officinalis)
Calendula (Calendula officinalis)
California Poppy (Eschscholtzia californica)
Carnation or Pinks (Dianthus spp.)
Cattail (Typha latifolia)
Chamomile (Matricaria chamomilla or Anthemis nobilis)
Chickweed (Stellaria media)
Chicory (Cichorium intybus)
Chives (Allium schoenoprasum)
Chrysanthemum (Chrysanthemum morifolium)
Cilantro (Coriandrum sativum)
Clover, Red (Trifolium pratense)
Cornflower/Bachelor Buttons (Centaurea cyanus)
Daisy, English (Bellis perennis)
Dandelion (Taraxacum officinalis)
Day Lily (Hemerocallis spp.)
Dill (Anethum graveolens)
Elder (Sambucus canadensis)
Fennel (Foeniculum vulgare)
Feverfew (Chrysanthemum parthenium)
Forget-Me-Nots (Myosotis alpestris)
Fuschia (Fuschia spp.)
Garlic Chives (Allium tuberosum)
Geranium (Geranium spp.)
Gladiolas (Gladiolus spp.)
Goldenrod (Solidago spp.)
Hawthorn (Crataegus spp.)
Hibiscus (Hibiscus rosa-sinensis) NOT THE"BLUE
   HIBISCUS" WHICH IS NOT A TRUE HIBISCUS
Hollyhock (Althea resea)
Honeysuckle (Lonicera spp.)
Hyssop (Hyssopus officinalis)
Jasmine (Jasminum spp.) NOT TO BE CONFUSED
   WITH TOXIC YELLOW CAROLINA JESSAMINE
Johnny-Jump-Up (Viola tricolor)
Lavender (Lavandula officinalis)

Lemon Balm (Melissa officinalis)
Lemon Blossom (Citrus limon)
Lemon Verbena (Aloysia triphylla)
Lilac (Syringa vulgaris)
Magnolia (Magnolia grandiflora or denudata)
Mallow (Malva neglecta)
Marjoram (Origanum majorana)
Marshmallow (Althea officinalis)
Mints (Mentha spp.)
Mullein (Verbascum spp.)
Mustard (Brassica spp.)
Nasturtium (Tropaeolum majus)
Orange Blossom (Citrus sinensis)
Oregano (Origanum vulgare)
Pansy (Viola spp.)
Pelargonium/ Scented geraniums (Pelargon ium spp.)
Petunia (Petunia hybrida)
Pineapple Guava (Feijoa sellowiana)
Pineapple Sage (Salvia spp.)
Plum Blossom (Prunus spp.)
Primrose (Primula vulgaris)
Rose (Rosa spp.)
Rosemary (Rosmarinum officinalis)
Safflowers (Carthamus tictorius)
Sage (Salvia spp.)
Snapdragon (Antirrhinum majus)
Society Garlic (Tuhlbaghia violacea)
Squash Blossom (Cucurbita spp.)
Stocks (Matthiola sp.)
Sunflower (Helianthus annuus)
Sweet Violets (Viola odorata) NOT TO BE CONFUSED
    WITH TOXIC AFRICAN VIOLETS
Sweet Woodruff (Galium odorata)
Thistle (Cirsium spp.)
Thyme (Thymus spp.)
Tulip (Tulipa spp.)

Wild Radish (Raphanus sativus)
Yarrow (Achillea millefolium)
Yucca (Yucca spp.)

The following flowers are very toxic and should not be used around food in any way, not even for decoration. This is a partial list. In all cases, be sure you positively know the flowers are non-toxic before ingesting them. Remember, "sweet smelling" does not mean "edible."

TOXIC FLOWERS include the following:
African Violet (Saintpaulia ionantha)
Arnica (Arnica montana)
Azalea, all varieties (Rhododendron spp.)
Autumn Crocus (Colchicum autumnale)
Bleeding Hearts (Dicentra spectabilis)
Broom (Cytisus scoparius)
Carolina Jessamine / Yellow Carolina Jasmine
    (Gelsemium sempervirens)
Daffodil (Narcissus pseudonarcissus)
Death Camas (Zigadenus spp.)
Delphinium (Delphinium spp.)
Flowering Indian Tobacco (Nicotiana glauca)
Foxglove (Digitalis purpurea)
Hydrangea (Hydrangea macrophylla)
Jimson Weed (Datura stramonium)
Larkspur (Dephinium ajacis)
Lupine (Lupinus spp.)
Monkshood (Aconitum columbianum or napellus)
Nightshade, black (Solanum americanum)
Nightshade, deadly (Atropa belladonna)
Nightshade, purple (Solanum dulcamara)
Oleander (Nerium oleander)
Poinsettia (Euphorbia pulcherrima)
Poison Hemlock (Conium maculatum)
Rhododendron, all varieties (Rhododendron spp.)

Sweet Peas (Lathyrus spp.)
Wisteria (Wisteria sinensis)

In addition, many common house plants and exotic tropical flowers are toxic. Be sure not to eat flowers that have been sprayed with pesticides (most florist's flowers) or ones that are growing right beside the road. Rub edible flowers on the wrist to determine extreme sensitivities; if you react, do not eat them. Use edible flowers in small quantities to avoid allergic reactions.

Edible flowers can be used in a variety of ways to add beauty and flavor to your foods. Pick them shortly before using, and if you must store them in the refrigerator, be sure to keep them moist. Here are some delicious ideas:

**Garnish stir fries, salads and dips with nasturtiums, opal basil, borage, pansies and violets.

**Stuff the large blossoms of hollyhock, hibiscus, day lily, and squash with tofu salad or cottage cheese. These can also be breaded and fried.

**Use chive and onion flowers, separated into flowerettes for a spicy addition to soups, salads and egg omelettes.

**Sprinkle your fruit salad with sweet blossoms from rose geranium, pineapple guava, apple, orange or borage.

**Flavor honeys by soaking fragrant blossoms such as lavender, roses, jasmine, honeysuckle or violets in mild honey in the sun for 1-2 weeks. The flowers can remain in the honey. Use on waffles, muffins and in herb teas.

**Garnish the top of gelatin or agar desserts with johnny-jump-ups and sweet alyssums just before they get firm.

**Add thyme flowers, day lily buds, chrysanthemums or calendula petals to soups.

**Float borage and pineapple sage flowers in drinks, fresh, or frozen into ice cubes.

**Spice up your tea party sandwiches with nasturtium and mustard flowers. Let the nasturtiums show on the edges for added beauty.

**Make fruit sauces with lemon, mint or nutmeg geraniums. Use leaves and flowers.

**Flavor vinegars with thyme, chive, nasturtium and dill flowers by soaking in a warm place for 4-6 weeks.

**Add finely diced calendula, hyssop or other bright flower to pancake batter, cheese spread or herb butter.

**Decorate a special cake with honeysuckle, fuschia and mint flowers.

The ways of enjoying edible flowers are endless. May this serve as a springboard for your creativity, and inspiration for a multitude of culinary delights from your flower garden.

GLOSSARY OF SPECIAL FOODS

AVAILABLE IN ORIENTAL MARKET OR CHINESE HERB STORE:

Aduki Bean (Red Bean) - small bean that benefits kidney

Bean Curd Skin or Sticks - available in dried form, made by removing the layer that forms on the top of soy milk

Black Beans (Salted or Dried) - used as a seasoning, benefits kidney

Black Fungus - available dried (SEE HERB APPENDIX)

Black Sesame Seeds - look similar to brown ones but black; often have small rocks in them so be sure to clean well

Burdock Root (Gobo in Japanese market) - used similar to carrot

Chestnuts (dried or fresh) - large nut requiring cooking to be edible

Chinese Miso (Fermented Bean Curd) - available in a jar, not refrigerated; used as a salty seasoning

Chinese Mushrooms (Black or Shitake) - a mainstay of Chinese vegetarian cooking, these come dried and must be soaked prior to use. The soak water makes a delicious cooking water. The thicker, more expensive ones have a richer flavor. The stems remain tough and can be removed when dry, powdered and used as seasoning.

Five Spice Powder (SEE HERB APPENDIX)

Ginger Root (Fresh or Pickled) - fresh appearance is a knobby root, pickled will come in a jar and vary in looks.

Hair Seaweed - looks like dry, fine black hair; soak before use.

Jujube Date - red Chinese date (SEE HERB APPENDIX)

Kombu - available dry in wide pieces; this is what is usually sold in Chinese markets labelled simply as "Dried Seaweed." Soak before use.

Lotus Root - light brown root that has holes running lengthwise through it. (SEE HERB APPENDIX)

Lily Bulbs - small white crescent shaped roots that come dry (SEE HERB APPENDIX)

Lily Flowers - available dry, look like golden to brown, short noodles

Mung Bean (Green Bean) - available dry or sprouted or made into noodles called bean threads.

Mustard Stem Pickle - usually in a vacuum packed plastic package, used as a salty seasoning

Nori - available as dry, black or dark green sheets of seaweed, used to roll or wrap rice, vegetable, etc.

Salted Duck Egg - preserved eggs that need to be boiled.

Soybean Film - available in the freezer, used as a wrapping

Straw Mushrooms - occasionally available dry or fresh, usually canned

Sweet Rice Flour - also called mochi flour, used as a thickener

Taro Root - these vary in size with the large ones having a better flavor and have a hairy outer skin that must be peeled away. Some people have a sensitivity to taro and must wear gloves when preparing.

Tofu Cake (Baked Tofu) - pre-seasoned, pressed and baked; appears light brown in color. Plain tofu is white in appearance and usually packed in water.

Toasted Sesame Oil - made from toasted brown sesame seeds, used as a seasoning for its distinctive rich flavor

Wakame - a dried, leafy green seaweed; soak before use

Wax Gourd Peel - comes pressed into a block; used in soups (SEE HERB APPENDIX)

White Fungus - available dried, looks like silvery flowers (SEE HERB APPENDIX)

Winter Melon - pale green melon, cooked similar to a winter squash; diuretic in function

AVAILABLE IN NATURAL FOOD STORES AND LARGE SUPERMARKETS:

Arrowroot - white powdered root used as thickening. Dissolve in cold water first and do not boil

Bragg's Liquid Aminos - a salty seasoning with less sodium than soy sauce

Brown Rice Syrup - used similar to honey; less sweet

Cilantro - also known as Chinese parsley or Mexican parsley, do not cook as it loses its flavor

Couscous - prepared from durum wheat, cooks in 5 minutes

Daikon Radish - long white radish, used like carrot

Ghee - clarified butter. Can be prepared by slowly boiling regular butter until a light golden oil remains; strain out the solids and the remaining oil is ghee.

Gluten Flour - the protein portion from wheat flour, used to make meat substitutes. Sometime prepared gluten is available and may be called seitan.

Hiziki - dried black, noodle like seaweed; soak before use

Jicama - light brown, round root with juicy white flesh; can be used raw or cooked

Kaboche Squash - a variety of winter squash with green skin and orange inside. The skin is edible when cooked.

Millet - tiny yellow grain

Miso - a salty fermented seasoning made from soybeans, sea salt and sometimes a grain

Oat Bran - popularly used to lower cholesterol; very mild taste

Quinoa - a tiny grain from South America, high in protein

Sweet Brown Rice - used as a thickener or to make mochi

Tempeh - a fermented soybean product, usually found in the freezer section; requires thorough cooking before use

Tofu - a soy bean product made from soy bean milk, available unseasoned, packed in water, or pressed, seasoned and baked.

Umeboshi Plum - a salty, pickled plum, used as seasoning and after meals to improve digestion

Index of Recipes

MATERIALS ON TAOIST HEALTH, ARTS AND SCIENCES

BOOKS

The Tao of Nutrition by Maoshing Ni, Ph.D., with Cathy McNease, B.S., M.H. - Working from ancient Chinese medical classics and contemporary research, Dr. Maoshing Ni and Cathy McNease have compiled an indispensable guide to natural healing. This exceptional book shows the reader how to take control of one's health through one's eating habits. This volume contains 3 major sections: the first section deals with theories of Chinese nutrition and philosophy; the second describes over 100 common foods in detail, listing their energetic properties, therapeutic actions and individual remedies. The third section lists nutritional remedies for many common ailments. This book presents both a healing system and a disease prevention system which is flexible in adapting to every individual's needs. 214 pages. Stock No. BNUTR. Softcover, $14.50

Chinese Vegetarian Delights by Lily Chuang
An extraordinary collection of recipes based on principles of traditional Chinese nutrition. Many recipes are therapeutically prepared with herbs. Diet has long been recognized as a key factor in health and longevity. For those who require restricted diets and those who choose an optimal diet, this cookbook is a rare treasure. Meat, sugar, diary products and fried foods are excluded. Produce, grains, tofu, eggs and seaweeds are imaginatively prepared. 104 pages. Stock No. BCHIV. Softcover, $7.50

Chinese Herbology Made Easy - by Maoshing Ni, Ph.D.
This text provides an overview of Oriental medical theory, in-depth descriptions of each herb category, with over 300 black and white photographs, extensive tables of individual herbs for easy reference, and an index of pharmaceutical and Pin-Yin names. The distillation of overwhelming material into essential elements enables one to focus efficiently and develop a clear understanding of Chinese herbology. This book is especially helpful for those studying for their California Acupuncture License. 202 pages. Stock No. BCHIH. Softcover, 14.50

Crane Style Chi Gong Book - By Daoshing Ni, Ph.D.
Chi Gong is a set of meditative exercises that was developed several thousand years ago by Taoists in China. It is now practiced for healing purposes, combining breathing techniques, body movements and mental imagery to guide the smooth flow of energy throughout the body. This book gives a more detailed account and study of Chi Gong than the videotape alone. It may be used with or without the videotape. Includes complete instructions and information on using Chi Gong exercise as a medical therapy. 55 pages. Stock No. BCRAN. Spiral bound $10.95

VIDEO TAPES

Attune Your Body with Dao-In: Taoist Exercise for a Long and Happy Life (VHS) - by Master Ni. Dao-In is a series of typical Taoist movements which are traditionally used for physical energy conducting. These exercises were passed down from the ancient achieved Taoists and immortals. The ancients discovered that Dao-In exercises not only solved problems of stagnant energy, but also increased their health and lengthened their years. The exercises are also used as practical support for cultivation and the higher achievements of spiritual immortality. Master Ni, Hua-Ching, heir to the tradition of the achieved masters, is the first one who releases this important Taoist practice to the modern world in this 1 hour videotape. Stock No. VDAOI VHS $59.95

T'ai Chi Chuan: An Appreciation (VHS) - by Master Ni - Different styles of T'ai Chi Ch'uan as Movement have different purposes and accomplish different results. In this long awaited videotape, Master Ni, Hua-Ching presents three styles of T'ai Chi Movement handed down to him through generations of highly developed masters. They are the "Gentle Path," "Sky Journey," and "Infinite Expansion" styles of T'ai Chi Movement. The three styles are presented uninterrupted in this unique videotape and are set to music for observation and appreciation. Stock No. VAPPR. VHS 30 minutes $49.95

Crane Style Chi Gong (VHS) - by Dr. Daoshing Ni, Ph.D.
Chi Gong is a set of meditative exercises developed several thousand years ago by ancient Taoists in China. It is now practiced for healing stubborn chronic diseases, strengthening the body to prevent disease and as a tool for further spiritual enlightenment. It combines breathing techniques, simple body movements, and mental imagery to guide the smooth flow of energy throughout the body. Chi gong is easy to learn for all ages. Correct and persistent practice will increase one's energy, relieve stress or tension, improve concentration and clarity, release emotional stress and restore general well-being. 2 hours Stock No. VCRAN. $65.95

Eight Treasures (VHS) - By Maoshing Ni, Ph.D.
These exercises help open blocks in a person's energy flow and strengthen one's vitality. It is a complete exercise combining physical stretching and toning and energy conducting movements coordinated with breathing. The Eight Treasures are an exercise unique to the Ni family. Patterned from nature, its 32 movements are an excellent foundation for Tai Chi Chuan or martial arts. 1 hour, 45 minutes. Stock No. VEIGH. $49.95

Tai Chi Chuan I & II (VHS) - By Maoshing Ni, Ph.D.
This exercise integrates the flow of physical movement with that of integral energy in the Taoist style of "Harmony," similar to the long form of Yang-style Tai Chi Chuan. Tai Chi has been practiced for thousands of years to help both physical longevity and spiritual cultivation. 1 hour each. Each Video Tape $49.95. Order both for $90.00. Stock Nos: Part I, VTAI1; Part II, VTAI2; Set of two, VTAI3.

AUDIO CASSETTES

Invocations: Health and Longevity and Healing a Broken Heart - By Maoshing Ni, Ph.D. *Updated with additional material!* This audio cassette guides the listener through a series of ancient invocations to channel and conduct one's own healing energy and vital force. "Thinking is louder than thunder." The mystical power by which all miracles are brought about is your sincere practice of this principle. 30 minutes. Stock No. AINVO. $9.95

Chi Gong for Stress Release - By Maoshing Ni, Ph.D.
This audio cassette guides you through simple, ancient breathing exercises that enable you to release day-to-day stress and tension that are such a common cause of illness today. 30 minutes. Stock No. ACHIS. $9.95

Chi Gong for Pain Management - By Maoshing Ni, Ph.D.
Using easy visualization and deep-breathing techniques that have been developed over thousands of years, this audio cassette offers methods for overcoming pain by invigorating your energy flow and unblocking obstructions that cause pain. 30 minutes. Stock No. ACHIP. $9.95

Tao Teh Ching Cassette Tapes
This classic work of Lao Tzu has been recorded in this two-cassette set that is a companion to the book translated by Master Ni. Professionally recorded and read by Robert Rudelson. 120 minutes. Stock No. ATAOT. $12.95

Order Master Ni's book, *The Complete Works of Lao Tzu,* and Tao Teh Ching Cassette Tapes for only $23.00. Stock No. ABTAO.

Books in English By Master Ni

New Publications
Ageless Counsel for Modern Life - $15.95
The Mystical Universal Mother - $14.95
Moonlight in the Dark Night - $12.95
Harmony - The Art of Life - $14.95
Internal Growth Through Tao - $13.95
Power of Natural Healing - $14.95
Essence of Universal Spirituality - $19.95
Guide to Inner Light - $12.95
Nurture Your Spirits - $12.95
The Key to Good Fortune: Refining Your Spirit - $12.95
Quest of Soul - $11.95
Eternal Light - $14.95
Attune Your Body with Dao-In - $14.95

Beginning Readings
Stepping Stones for Spiritual Success - $12.95
The Gentle Path of Spiritual Progress - $12.95
Spiritual Messages from a Buffalo Rider - $12.95
8,000 Years of Wisdom, Volume I and II - Each $12.50, Both $22.00

Taoist Classics and Esoteric Teachings
Book of Changes and Unchanging Truth - hardcover $35.00
The Complete Works of Lao Tzu - $12.95
The Taoist Inner View of the Universe - $14.95
Tao, the Subtle Universal Law - $7.50
Attaining Unlimited Life (Chuang Tzu) - paper $18.00, Hardcover $25.00
The Heavenly Way - $2.50
The Story of Two Kingdoms - hardcover, $14.00
Quest of Soul - $11.95
Eternal Light - $14.95

Personal Vision and Practical Development
The Uncharted Voyage Towards the Subtle Light - $14.50
Footsteps of the Mystical Child - $9.50
Workbook for Spiritual Development - $12.50
Poster of Master Lu, Tung Ping - $10.95; with Workbook, $6.45 (2 shipping
    chgs.)
The Way of Integral Life - paper $14.00, hardcover $20.00
Enlightenment: Mother of Spiritual Independence - paper, $12.50,
    hardcover $22.00

How To Order

Name: _____

Address: _____

City: _____ State: _____ Zip: _____

Phone - Daytime: _____ Evening: _____

(We may telephone you if we have questions about your order.)

Qty.	Stock No.	Title/Description	Price Each	Total Price

Total amount for items ordered_____

Sales tax (CA residents only, 8-1/4%)_____

Shipping Charge (See below)_____

Total Amount Enclosed_____

Visa _____ Mastercard _____ Expiration Date _____

Card number:_____

Signature:_____

Shipping: In the US, we use UPS when possible. Please give full street address or nearest crossroads. All packages are insured at no extra charge. If shipping to more than one address, use separate shipping charges. Remember: 1 - 10 copies of Heavenly Way, Tao Teh Ching audio tapes and each book and tape are single items. Posters (up to 5 per tube) are a separate item. Please allow 2 - 4 weeks for US delivery and 6 - 10 weeks for foreign surface mail.

By Mail: Complete this form with payment (US funds only, No Foreign Postal Money Orders, please) and mail to: Union of Tao and Man, 1314 Second St. #A, Santa Monica, CA 90401

Phone Orders: (310) 576-1901 - You may leave credit card orders anytime on our answering machine. Please speak clearly and remember to leave your full name and daytime phone number. We will call only if we have a question with your order, there is a delay or you specifically ask for phone confirmation.

Inquiries: If you have questions concerning your order, please refer to the date and invoice number on the top center of your invoice to help us locate your order swiftly.

Shipping Charges -
Domestic Surface: First item $3.25, each additional, add $.50.
Canada Surface: First item $3.25, each additional, add $1.00.
Canada Air: First item $4.00, each additional, add $2.00
Foreign Surface: First Item $3.50, each additional, add $2.00.
Foreign Air: First item $12.00, each additional, add $7.00.

For the Trade: Wholesale orders may be placed direct to publisher, or with NewLeaf, BookPeople, The Distributors, Inland Books, GreatWay Quality Books in US; DeepBooks in Europe; Quest Book Trade Distributors in Australia.

Thank you for your order

Spiritual Study Through the College of Tao

The College of Tao and the Union of Tao and Man were established formally in California in the 1970's. This tradition is a very old spiritual culture of mankind, holding long experience of human spiritual growth. Its central goal is to offer healthy spiritual education to all people of our society. This time tested tradition values the spiritual development of each individual self and passes down its guidance and experience.

Master Ni carries his tradition from its country of origin to the west. He chooses to avoid making the mistake of old-style religions that have rigid establishments which resulted in fossilizing the delicacy of spiritual reality. Rather, he prefers to guide the teachings of his tradition as a school of no boundary rather than a religion with rigidity. Thus, the branches or centers of this Taoist school offer different programs of similar purpose. Each center extends its independent service, but all are unified in adopting Master Ni's work as the foundation of teaching to fulfill the mission of providing spiritual education to all people.

The centers offer their classes, teaching, guidance and practices on building the groundwork for cultivating a spiritually centered and well-balanced life. As a person obtains the correct knowledge with which to properly guide himself or herself, he or she can then become more skillful in handling the experiences of daily life. The assimilation of good guidance in one's practical life brings about different stages of spiritual development.

Any interested individual is welcome to join and learn to grow for oneself. Or you just might like to take a few classes in which you are interested. You might like to visit the center or take classes near where you live, or you yourself may be interested in organizing a center or study group based on the model of existing centers. In that way, we all work together for the spiritual benefit of all people. We do not require any religious type of commitment.

The College of Tao also offers a Self-Study program based on Master Ni's books and videotapes. The course outline and details of how to participate is given in his book, *The Golden Message*. The Self-Study program gives people an opportunity to study the learning of Tao at their own speed, who wish to study on their own or are too far from a center.

The learning is life. The development is yours. The connection of study may be helpful, useful and serviceable, directly to you.

- -

Mail to: Union of Tao and Man, 1314 Second Street #A, Santa Monica, CA 90401

_____ I wish to be put on the mailing list of the Union of Tao and Man to be notified of classes, educational activities and new publications.

Name:_____

Address:_____

City:_____State:_____Zip:_____

Herbs Used by Ancient Taoist Masters

The pursuit of everlasting youth or immortality throughout human history is an innate human desire. Long ago, Chinese esoteric Taoists went to the high mountains to contemplate nature, strengthen their bodies, empower their minds and develop their spirit. From their studies and cultivation, they gave China alchemy and chemistry, herbology and acupuncture, the I Ching, astrology, martial arts and T'ai Chi Chuan, Chi Gong and many other useful kinds of knowledge.

Most important, they handed down in secrecy methods for attaining longevity and spiritual immortality. There were different levels of approach; one was to use a collection of food herb formulas that were only available to highly achieved Taoist masters. They used these food herbs to increase energy and heighten vitality. This treasured collection of herbal formulas remained within the Ni family for centuries.

Now, through Traditions of Tao, the Ni family makes these foods available for you to use to assist the foundation of your own positive development. It is only with a strong foundation that expected results are produced from diligent cultivation.

As a further benefit, in concert with the Taoist principle of self-sufficiency, Traditions of Tao offers the food herbs along with the Union of Tao and Man's publications in a distribution opportunity for anyone serious about financial independence.

Send to: Traditions of Tao
1314 Second Street #A
Santa Monica, CA 90401

☐ Please send me a Traditions of Tao brochure.

☐ Please send me information on becoming an independent distributor of Traditions of Tao herbal products and publications.

Name _____

Address_____

City_____State_____Zip_____

Phone (day)_____(night)_____

Yo San University of Traditional Chinese Medicine

"Not just a medical career, but a life-time commitment to raising one's spiritual standard."

Thank you for your support and interest in our publications and services. It is by your patronage that we continue to offer you the practical knowledge and wisdom from this venerable Taoist tradition.

Because of your sustained interest in Taoism, we formed Yo San University of Traditional Chinese Medicine, a non-profit educational institute in January 1989 under the direction of founder Master Ni, Hua-Ching. Yo San University is the continuation of 38 generations of Ni family practitioners who handed down knowledge and wisdom from fathers to sons. Its purpose is to train and graduate practitioners of the highest caliber in Traditional Chinese Medicine, which includes acupuncture, herbology and spiritual development.

We view Traditional Chinese Medicine as the application of spiritual development. Its foundation is the spiritual capability to know life, to know a person's problem and how to cure it. We teach students how to care for themselves and others, and emphasize the integration of traditional knowledge and modern science. We offer a complete Master's degree program approved by the California State Department of Education that provides an excellent education in Traditional Chinese Medicine and meets all requirements for state licensure.

We invite you to inquire into our school about a creative and rewarding career as a holistic physician. Classes are also open to persons interested only in self-enrichment. For more information, please fill out the form below and send it to:

Yo San University,
1314 Second Street
Santa Monica, CA 90401

☐ Please send me information on the Masters degree program in Traditional Chinese Medicine.

☐ Please send me information on health workshops and seminars.

☐ Please send me information on continuing education for acupuncturists and health professionals.

Name _____

Address _____

City_____State_____Zip_____

Phone(day)_____(night)_____